Notes from the New Europe

A reporter's commentary and columns: 2007-2009

Susan Easton

NextGen Publishing Company
www.nextgenpub.net

First Edition published July, 2009.

Photography , cover and design by Erica Simone (www.ericasimone.com) and set in Minion Pro and Bell Gothic Std types.
Printed and bound in the United States of America and the United Kingdom.

Library of Congress Cataloging-in-Publication Data is on file with the Library of Congress.

Easton, Susan

Notes from the New Europe, A Reporter's Commentary and Columns: 2007-2009/ by Susan Easton
-1st ed.
p. cm.
Includes index.
ISBN-13: 078-0-9749694-2-8(paperback: alk. paper)
ISBN-10: 0-9749694-2-7 (paperback: alk. paper)

1. Title [1. Political Science - Essays. 2. Political Science - General]

FIRST PRINTING

NextGen Publishing Company
Burlingame, CA 94010
http://www.nextgenpub.net

Contents

Contents

Is Religion Futile? (Perhaps it is in London)

On March 26, in the Westminster Central Methodist Hall, the Times of London co-hosted a public debate. The proposition to be argued was "we'd all be better off without religion." The run-up to this event had taken on such a life of its own that by early March the British press had begun heralding the 26th as "Futility of Faith Day. " The nickname stuck. The event sold out.

The team debating "for" the proposition featured celebrity atheists, Richard Dawkins (author of the bestselling "The God Delusion") and Christopher Hitchens (Vanity Fair correspondent and author of the forthcoming rant, "God is Not Great.") Their point man was a lesser-known but witty philosopher named A.C. Grayling.

The team debating "against" the proposition (which is to say for religion) comprised a female Rabbi and two professors, neither of whom were theologians and both of whom owned up to being lapsed Methodists. Not exactly an all-star God squad.

Curiously (or not), neither team had a representative from the Muslim faith. One presumes The Times did not want to take that risk. Upon reflection in her post debate coverage, the religion reporter for the Times, Ruth Gledhill, also mused that no one had been tasked with providing a definition of "religion" before the debate ensued. The devil is in the details.

Christopher Hitchens opened the case against religion using what he termed "the Sesame Street System." Naming a bevy of world locations all beginning with a "B" (Baghdad, Beirut, Bosnia, etc.), Hitchens immodestly noted that he'd been to every one of them and that faith-based conflicts, genocides, racial cleansing, and wars had ruined them all. Religion, in the form of cultural identity, Hitchens asserted, leads people to kill one another and one another's children based on the kind of Christian or Muslim one was. Hence the troubles in Northern Ireland and now, he fumed, one saw that Sunnis and Shiites were engaged in retaliatory torchings of one another's mosques in Iraq. The warring parties of God have replaced the totalitarian regime of Saddam, he lamented. When would we learn , he bemoaned, that religions were not divine revelations sent down from heaven, rather man-created and thus prone to human failures. Reminding any "God botherers" in the audience that humans were one half of a chromosome away from chimps, what business did they have forming these destructive philosophical systems, Hitchens demanded? "People who tell you they know what God's will is are your enemies," he concluded and sat down to generous applause. He obviously has an evangelical fervor which moves the masses.

Nigel Spivey loosed the first salvo from the "against" team. Spivey makes his living in the academic worlds of archaeology and anthropology. As his best-known BBC documentary program was entitled "Digging For Jesus," it was no surprise that Spivey took the long view. Religion, Spivey put it to the audience, began with the onset of ritualistic burials and cave paintings 40,000 years ago. Then he made a mad dash up to the present, citing cultural achievements throughout the ages as proof that humanity was hard-wired for transcendent expressions. Not following strict Cambridge rules for such events, Spivey's summing up point was that debating the futility of faith was a waste of time. The "the sea of faith would roll on," he waxed poetically, "providing a force by which humans could survive." This may have been a coded message since most Brits would recognize the sea of faith as an association of "progressive Christians," founded in part by Anglican priests who confessed to not believing in God at all, but still kept their jobs.

Next up was Richard Dawkins, literary darling and smug atheist icon. Dawkins began by lashing out at any notion of a "gene" for faith and characterized adults who needed to believe in religion as grown-ups "sucking on dummies" (that's Brit-speak for a baby pacifier). After this outburst of pure petulance, in a revealing aside, Dawkins boasted that religion was not a part of his nature, nor that of any of his friends in universities. Dawkins had his own metaphor on offer. He spent the rest of his allotted time comparing religion to a computer firewall. It blocked out the flow of ideas and thus was no friend of science and progress. As for inspiring the arts, what kind of ceiling would Michelangelo have painted on the cathedral of science if his patrons had been scientists and not Popes, he wondered, a query often asked by the wholly enlightened.

Rabbi Julia Neuberger, credited in the program as a broadcaster and a "social reformer," began by sharing her bona fides. She aligned herself with the audience by telling them that she was liberal to the point of nearly falling off the (left) edge. Portraying Jewish theology as "inconsistent," the Rabbi depicted Jews as a religious people who lived their lives through the observance of sacred holidays and rituals. Dependence on a personal God was not a criterion for being neither a good Jew. What mattered was how a life was lived. It all had to do with inspiration, with modesty, and with humility. Religion was, therefore, a universal because it under girded social justice and was therefore was to be tolerated --even by the most rabid anti-religionist -- the activist Rabbi instructed.

Closing arguments on behalf of the "for" team were handled by A.C. Grayling. In a newspaper interview published before the debate, Grayling described believers as "being away with the fairies." But rather than being dismissive when on stage, Grayling turned out to have the best allegory of the night. He asked the audience to imagine a martian scholar who had spent lifetime studying the Earth's religions, with a specialist degree in Christianity. The martian decides he needs to do some field work and has "a sort of Scotty person" beam him down to our planet, but not without first taking care to pinpoint his place of arrival. The martian was keen not be beamed into any of those "B" places, mentioned earlier by Hitchens, because he did not want to end up being tortured or shot as a part of his research. Once he was settled at a coffee shop in London's Waterloo Station, the martian started to engage (clueless) travelers in Q and A. His basic inquiry involved what these individuals would want for their children. The answers included personal happiness, social status, job fulfillment, and love. The martian professed amazement because he had read the New Testament and it said things like blessed are those who mourn, and don't worry about tomorrow, and give away your possessions because a rich man can't get into heaven. How could Christianity be a real religion if its practitioners didn't want their children to become… well? Christians. The audience seemed to enjoy Grayling's fairy tale approach; fairy tales being a description of Bible-based faith employed by many a non-believer.

Batting clean-up for the A-team was Professor and philosopher Roger Scruton, an eloquent and respected gentleman. Perhaps prejudicing anyone in the audience not familiar with his serious writings, the evening's handout program described Scruton as running "an experimental farm in Wiltshire which turns grass into ideas and ideas into feelings." Hmm… In the end, Scruton placed the blame for people who didn't see the need for religion on Plato's lofty idealism. Although he earnestly believed that humankind could exist on a diet of pure philosophy and reason, that just wasn't so, said the grass farmer. Humans yearn in their lives. The yearnings are not always rational, but they are often spiritual in nature. Therefore, religion can't be done away with because the victims of that crime would be our inspirations and aspirations.

And so the arguments ended, but the audience had lots of comments after the formal debate. When the circus was ready to leave the hall, a second and final vote was taken (there was a predebate vote which is required by strict debating procedure.) Not surprisingly, the motion carried by 427 votes.

Here are the numbers:

- 1205 or 57.6% for the motion (better off without religion)
- 778 or 37.4% against the motion (better off with religion)
- 100 or 5.0% undecided

Talk is now underway about another debate in which heavyweight Christians can be brought in for the pro-faith platform to balance the atheist fundamentalism of Dawkins and Hitchens.

About the Author:

Susan Easton is the European Correspondent for Human Events, the national conservative newspaper published from Washington, D.C. since 1944.

Both a journalist and theologian by training, Ms. Easton brings her unique prospective to her popular commentaries on the contemporary European political and cultural scene. Her timely columns cover current affairs, politics, religion, and society throughout the EU and the United Kingdom.

This collection is from the critical period of 2007 through mid-2009.

Ms. Easton's articles are also published on-line at : http://www.HumanEvents.com.

Contents

Contents

Is Religion Futile? (Perhaps it is in London)

On March 26, in the Westminster Central Methodist Hall, the Times of London co-hosted a public debate. The proposition to be argued was "we'd all be better off without religion." The run-up to this event had taken on such a life of its own that by early March the British press had begun heralding the 26th as "Futility of Faith Day. " The nickname stuck. The event sold out.

The team debating "for" the proposition featured celebrity atheists, Richard Dawkins (author of the bestselling "The God Delusion") and Christopher Hitchens (Vanity Fair correspondent and author of the forthcoming rant, "God is Not Great.") Their point man was a lesser-known but witty philosopher named A.C. Grayling.

The team debating "against" the proposition (which is to say for religion) comprised a female Rabbi and two professors, neither of whom were theologians and both of whom owned up to being lapsed Methodists. Not exactly an all-star God squad.

Curiously (or not), neither team had a representative from the Muslim faith. One presumes The Times did not want to take that risk. Upon reflection in her post debate coverage, the religion reporter for the Times, Ruth Gledhill, also mused that no one had been tasked with providing a definition of "religion" before the debate ensued. The devil is in the details.

Christopher Hitchens opened the case against religion using what he termed "the Sesame Street System." Naming a bevy of world locations all beginning with a "B" (Baghdad, Beirut, Bosnia, etc.), Hitchens immodestly noted that he'd been to every one of them and that faith-based conflicts, genocides, racial cleansing, and wars had ruined them all. Religion, in the form of cultural identity, Hitchens asserted, leads people to kill one another and one another's children based on the kind of Christian or Muslim one was. Hence the troubles in Northern Ireland and now, he fumed, one saw that Sunnis and Shiites were engaged in retaliatory torchings of one another's mosques in Iraq. The warring parties of God have replaced the totalitarian regime of Saddam, he lamented. When would we learn , he bemoaned, that religions were not divine revelations sent down from heaven, rather man-created and thus prone to human failures. Reminding any "God botherers" in the audience that humans were one half of a chromosome away from chimps, what business did they have forming these destructive philosophical systems, Hitchens demanded? "People who tell you they know what God's will is are your enemies," he concluded and sat down to generous applause. He obviously has an evangelical fervor which moves the masses.

Nigel Spivey loosed the first salvo from the "against" team. Spivey makes his living in the academic worlds of archaeology and anthropology. As his best-known BBC documentary program was entitled "Digging For Jesus," it was no surprise that Spivey took the long view. Religion, Spivey put it to the audience, began with the onset of ritualistic burials and cave paintings 40,000 years ago. Then he made a mad dash up to the present, citing cultural achievements throughout the ages as proof that humanity was hard-wired for transcendent expressions. Not following strict Cambridge rules for such events, Spivey's summing up point was that debating the futility of faith was a waste of time. The "the sea of faith would roll on," he waxed poetically, "providing a force by which humans could survive." This may have been a coded message since most Brits would recognize the sea of faith as an association of "progressive Christians," founded in part by Anglican priests who confessed to not believing in God at all, but still kept their jobs.

Next up was Richard Dawkins, literary darling and smug atheist icon. Dawkins began by lashing out at any notion of a "gene" for faith and characterized adults who needed to believe in religion as grown-ups "sucking on dummies" (that's Brit-speak for a baby pacifier). After this outburst of pure petulance, in a revealing aside, Dawkins boasted that religion was not a part of his nature, nor that of any of his friends in universities. Dawkins had his own metaphor on offer. He spent the rest of his allotted time comparing religion to a computer firewall. It blocked out the flow of ideas and thus was no friend of science and progress. As for inspiring the arts, what kind of ceiling would Michelangelo have painted on the cathedral of science if his patrons had been scientists and not Popes, he wondered, a query often asked by the wholly enlightened.

Rabbi Julia Neuberger, credited in the program as a broadcaster and a "social reformer," began by sharing her bona fides. She aligned herself with the audience by telling them that she was liberal to the point of nearly falling off the (left) edge. Portraying Jewish theology as "inconsistent," the Rabbi depicted Jews as a religious people who lived their lives through the observance of sacred holidays and rituals. Dependence on a personal God was not a criterion for being neither a good Jew. What mattered was how a life was lived. It all had to do with inspiration, with modesty, and with humility. Religion was, therefore, a universal because it under girded social justice and was therefore was to be tolerated --even by the most rabid anti-religionist -- the activist Rabbi instructed.

Closing arguments on behalf of the "for" team were handled by A.C. Grayling. In a newspaper interview published before the debate, Grayling described believers as "being away with the fairies." But rather than being dismissive when on stage, Grayling turned out to have the best allegory of the night. He asked the audience to imagine a martian scholar who had spent lifetime studying the Earth's religions, with a specialist degree in Christianity. The martian decides he needs to do some field work and has "a sort of Scotty person" beam him down to our planet, but not without first taking care to pinpoint his place of arrival. The martian was keen not be beamed into any of those "B" places, mentioned earlier by Hitchens, because he did not want to end up being tortured or shot as a part of his research. Once he was settled at a coffee shop in London's Waterloo Station, the martian started to engage (clueless) travelers in Q and A. His basic inquiry involved what these individuals would want for their children. The answers included personal happiness, social status, job fulfillment, and love. The martian professed amazement because he had read the New Testament and it said things like blessed are those who mourn, and don't worry about tomorrow, and give away your possessions because a rich man can't get into heaven. How could Christianity be a real religion if its practitioners didn't want their children to become… well? Christians. The audience seemed to enjoy Grayling's fairy tale approach; fairy tales being a description of Bible-based faith employed by many a non-believer.

Batting clean-up for the A-team was Professor and philosopher Roger Scruton, an eloquent and respected gentleman. Perhaps prejudicing anyone in the audience not familiar with his serious writings, the evening's handout program described Scruton as running "an experimental farm in Wiltshire which turns grass into ideas and ideas into feelings." Hmm… In the end, Scruton placed the blame for people who didn't see the need for religion on Plato's lofty idealism. Although he earnestly believed that humankind could exist on a diet of pure philosophy and reason, that just wasn't so, said the grass farmer. Humans yearn in their lives. The yearnings are not always rational, but they are often spiritual in nature. Therefore, religion can't be done away with because the victims of that crime would be our inspirations and aspirations.

And so the arguments ended, but the audience had lots of comments after the formal debate. When the circus was ready to leave the hall, a second and final vote was taken (there was a pre-debate vote which is required by strict debating procedure.) Not surprisingly, the motion carried by 427 votes.

Here are the numbers:

- 1205 or 57.6% for the motion (better off without religion)
- 778 or 37.4% against the motion (better off with religion)
- 100 or 5.0% undecided

Talk is now underway about another debate in which heavyweight Christians can be brought in for the pro-faith platform to balance the atheist fundamentalism of Dawkins and Hitchens.

How would you have voted? In days of yore, what was said and by whom at such events was a closed circle. Thanks to the Internet, one can download the audio and listen to the banter, slings, and arrows of this debate for one's self. In addition to the pod cast option, there are over 40 pages of blog entries posted to the original Ruth Gledhill/Times article on The Futility of Faith Debate. Click on the toolbar option "Comment." When that page comes up, look to the right and click on "Faith."

April 9, 2007

Why England Isn't Easter Island

Listeners to BBC's "Radio 4" could be forgiven for thinking that an evil British Broadcasting Corporation programmer had substituted a wicked satire for the scheduled Lenten Talk. On April 4th, in the middle of Holy Week, the Very Rev. Jeffrey Johns, Dean of St. Albans, took to the national airwaves and delivered an hysterical, if not heretical, diatribe.

"What sort of God was this," Johns huffed indignantly, "getting so angry with the world and the people he created and then, to calm himself down, demanding the blood of his own son? And anyway, why should God forgive us through punishing somebody else? It was worse than illogical, it was insane. It made God sound like a psychopath. If any human being behaved like this, we would say they were a monster."

Across the United Kingdom, there must have been an audible sucking noise as people drew in a collective horrified breath. Even a secular humanist with a two by four chip on his or her shoulder would have thought twice about calling God a psychopath on the eve of Good Friday. Many in the radio audience undoubtedly assumed that Jeffrey Johns was the latest Brit to come down with some screaming form of religious mania.

But the fact is that Johns didn't just burst into the Radio 4 studios, grab a microphone, and start his Freudian spew. He had been invited to editorialize on the meaning of Easter by the Religion Department at the BBC, a once revered institution which now stands accused of having adopted an anti-Christian agenda.

By way of background, in 2001, two months before 9-11, the BBC appointed Alan Bookbinder as the head of its Religion Department. Breaking with a tradition dating back to 1933, Bookbinder was the first person in this post to declare himself "an open-hearted agnostic." His predecessors were all practicing Christians, many of them ordained clergy. Indicative of their theological timidity, reactions to this appointment by the majority of the church's hierarchy were generally tepid. They were moved to characterize Bookbinder's ascension to the top of the religion division as "not reassuring." But surely this incident adds to suspicions about the Beeb's motives in matters of faith because this tempest was not inadvertently created in a teapot.

The Rev. Jeffrey Johns is a known ecclesiastical persona. He was forced to step down as Bishop of Reading in 2003 when it emerged that he was a homosexual, albeit a self-proclaimed "inactive" one. In a previous public statement, Johns' declared that, by age 10, he found that the Christian theory of penal substitution was -- as an explanation for the Crucifixion - "pretty repulsive and nonsensical." Is it indelicate to wonder if these two things are somehow connected?

Thankfully, there was an uproar over the Rev. John's commentary on the state of God's mental health. Newspapers reported that "evangelicals," (as opposed to the more accurate term "traditionalists") were "outraged" at this latest attempt by a member of the liberal wing of the church to hasten the demise of Christianity in England. Several unnamed Bishops were rumored to have opined that Johns' performance illustrated why he would have made a terrible Bishop, regardless of his sexual preferences. Good call.

One Bishop added his personal hope that Johns would "speedily reconsider and repent of his attack on apostolic Christianity." Hope springs eternal.

Just as robotically, the BBC reiterated its policy: "Lenten Talks are short individual authored opinions in which a contributor is invited to reflect on a different part of Christ's passion." But there must have been a bit of squirming behind the scenes because the Rev. Jeffrey Johns was given the opportunity to add two lines of clarification to his "talk" before it was aired (which means it was pre-recorded, not live and uncensored.)

In his murky mini-apologia, Johns stated that "Jesus died on the cross for our sins, but the price of those sins was paid by God, not to God." It's obviously all down to bad parenting and some Biblical bookkeeping in the gospel according to Jeffrey Johns.

Meanwhile, the 2007 Easter controversy in England intensified on another front. Chocolate. Somerfield's, a grocery chain equivalent to Safeway in the US, had commissioned Godiva Inc. to manufacture a special line of Easter Eggs. Unfortunately, the Somerfield's Press Office was suffering a crisis in salvific copy writing. The Godiva Eggs were introduced to a hungry public as a traditional gift exchanged to "celebrate the birth of Jesus." Pause. Yes, the birth of Jesus. Catching that little slip, a second press release attempted to correct the disinformation. No, went version two, Easter Eggs actually celebrated the "re-birth of Jesus." At this juncture the Church of England Press Office leapt into action. After some negotiating over terminology, a third press release appeared, but at that point the masses were far beyond caring. However, in a terse addendum to the third release, a Church of England spokesperson declared: "Easter is as hollow as a chocolate egg if one does not understand the meaning of the death and resurrection of Jesus."

Well, Amen, but from whence ought such understanding to come? Perhaps this chap does not recall the days when British children were taught, in their parish churches, that rolling eggs down a hill symbolized the stone which had been rolled away from the entrance to the tomb. It was about the spiritual, not about the sugar.

But all was not lost. Hallelujah. A vibrant Eastertide message DID turn up in -- of all places -- a weekend newspaper section devoted to listing alternative family activities. In exultation, up went the impassioned proclamation: Show Me The Bunny.

April 16, 2007

Pew Burning and the Perils of Pluralism

Mark your calendars. May 27th is Pluralism Sunday, so declared by The Center for Progressive Christianity (TCPG.org), an international network comprised of hundreds of affiliated congregations, representing many denominations, both in the USA and in England.

Pluralism Sunday event organizers are encouraging committed Christians to visit congregations other than their own. The idea here is that faith is not threatened, but indeed can be deepened, by exposure to other expressions of the same core beliefs. Among students of religious studies this practice is sometimes referred to as "cross training," pun intended.

Pluralism Sunday is also being promoted, in part, as an invitation to the unchurched, or to those who have rejected Christianity's long standing and often "wild" theological claims, to feel welcomed into worship communities and give the faith another go. Fair enough. But then come the assertions which make traditionalists and evangelicals uneasy.

One press release from TCPC states: "one does not need to believe that Jesus is the only way to God in order to be a Christian." This statement is used as part of the progressive inducement to visit a modern (or is that post-modern?) Christian church.

It also represents a profound misreading of the basic requirements for, among other things, membership in the World Council and also the National Council of Churches. Both of these theological organizations stipulate that, in order to be a member in good standing, a Christian congregation must recite The Nicene Creed and hold to the statements of faith therein.

Although there was a movement of those who wanted to work together across denominational divides as far back as the late 19th century, church leaders did not agree to establish a World Council of Churches until 1937. The actual formation was delayed by World War II. In August of 1948, representatives from 147 churches assembled in Amsterdam to write the seminal documents defining the WCC which, to this day, exclaims that it has "built new bridges over ancient chasms separating believers from one another." Show of hands. Does your denomination belong to the WCC? The Center for Progressive Christianity asserts: "There is a big difference between respectful politeness and an open-hearted open minded approach to people of other religious beliefs. There is a profound contradiction in claiming to have faith in a God who is greater than our ability to fully comprehend, and at the same time claiming that traditional Christianity is the only true faith in that God... We are called to worship God, not Christianity. What is divine is our encounter with God, something that is available to Christians and non-Christians alike."

It would then appear that Progressive Christians, however noble their intentions, are (ipso facto) self-defining as schismatics. They are ecclesiastical breakaways from the normative established Christian churches. They have used the Internet as the place upon which to nail their Reformational theses (a la Luther) to the virtual church door.

What Pluralism Sunday serves to illustrate is what happens when one champions a theological idea without reference to definitions and faith boundaries and absent thinking through the outcomes of a well-intentioned concept.

For a start, pluralism is to religion what multiculturalism is to society.

Multiculturalism, make no mistake, demands that you affirm the idea that each and every society is to be equally respected in the religious and cultural spheres. A child making his or her first communion is judged the same as the 12-year-old who, as witnessed in the news last week, cuts off the head of an infidel. Each pre-teen in this equation has done what God requires to show allegiance to a dogma.

If this concept creates an imbalance in your mind, consider the original ecclesiastical definition of pluralism. A Pluralist in the Church of England was one who held two or more congregational positions (known as benefices) at the same time. Clearly, in today's terms, pluralism has come to mean holding two contrary opinions in one's mind at the same time. According to F. Scott Fitzgerald this is also the definition of insanity.

When one floats comfortably down the stream of pluralism, here is what can be encountered along the way.

Muslims practicing polygamy, who apply for residence in England, are not only allowed to bring all their wives with them, but according to government policy ALL of their multiple wives are eligible for government-funded benefits. It's one for all and all for one even though bigamy is against the law in the UK.

The Hindu community in England are upset because they are, so far, not allowed to burn their dead on the same kind of open-air funeral pyres customary in India. Not a word, mind you, from the ecology camp on the environmental implications of torching your next of kin on a stack of the local British timber, the air quality be damned.

In Scotland, Muslims have requested that museums and libraries set aside a prayer room for adherents to the faith who regularly pray to Allah five times a day. In the spirit of pluralism, Muslims have, however, invited those of other faiths to use these prayer facilities whenever they please.

Since 2006, all new Church of England schools have been instructed that at least a quarter of their places are to be given to children from non-Christian families. But, oops, don't get caught recruiting for Christianity or you're off the faculty.

A week or so ago, a well known British architect made headlines by calling for all the empty Anglican parish churches in the English countryside to toss their pews on to the village green and setting them alight. His point was that these vacant places would serve the (assumed to be secular) populace better if they were converted into vibrant community centers, or at least into new post office branches.

The burgeoning Muslim community had a better idea. They are busy buying the old parish churches of England and converting them into mosques -- AND -- before you get too comfortable in casting aspersions on the Brits, take a look at the excellent work of Diana Eck. Her Pluralism Project, run out of Harvard University, will give you a wake-up call. On this website, you can look up your own city and state and see how many former venues of the Christian faith have been bought up and converted into worship places for a host of other religions.

What Pluralism means is that there is no need to call for the burning of pews. The market for Christian pews is falling. Bottoming out, so to speak. They are simply being tossed aside without having to be reduced to cinders. Are there demographic reasons for these changes? Of course. But does this mean that Pluralism is the future faith banner under which we all must march? Give it some thought.

Words have meanings. Just as one might read the label on a bottle of medication, or vitamins, or diet pills, it is an equally good idea to practice prescriptive theology. What's in the blend of ideas you swallow? Specific to this report -- what does it mean to join the ranks of Progressive Christians?

April 26, 2007

Horse Racing and the Handicapping of Gordon Brown

God Bless the Queen. She turned up in the U.S. to honor the 400th anniversary of the ill-fated Jamestown colony. Her Majesty is not known to enjoy presiding over commemorations of colonial failures. It was said that her affirmative RSVP came because the observance happily dovetailed with another famous event Elizabeth R has always longed to attend -- the Kentucky Derby. She's quite a pro in the horse business. The seven days of Royal races known as Ascot is surely the true holy week for the woman who also reigns over the Church of England

Tongues wagged that she was happy about her holiday schedule for reasons other than the promise of a Mint Julep by the weekend. On the day QE 2 arrived stateside, ballots were being cast throughout England, Scotland, and Wales. No big deal, one might think, for a woman who has seen plenty of politicos come and go in over 50 years on the throne. But her instincts must have tipped the Queen that this particular election was going to be a galloping big deal. And so it was.

In Wales, the Labour Party lost three seats, enough to force the other parties there to form a coalition government. In England, despite low voter turnout, the Conservatives won 870 English council seats. These gains, if fully translated at the next general election (expected to be called sometime in the next two years) would assure the Tories a win over Labour and bring about the election of David Cameron as Prime Minster. These will not be comforting thoughts for Gordon Brown who, for the past ten years, has been Tony Blair's understudy for that part.

Mr. Brown, a native of Scotland, must have awakened on Friday morning to the feeling that a cold and ominous wind was blowing down from the North. The Scottish National Party had finally gained majority status in their own Parliament, albeit by only one seat (47 to 46) over the Labour Party, ending 50 years of Labour running the show.

A bit of a history lesson is required to explain why this is another bad omen for Gordon Brown. May 2007 marks the 300th anniversary of the Act of Union. Under this agreement, England and Scotland were joined to establish The Kingdom of Great Britain (KGB). They pledged fealty to one monarch and blended their independent parliaments to create the Parliament of Great Britain. The center held, so to speak, until 1934 when the National Party of Scotland and the Scottish Party merged to form the Scottish National Party. The SNP won their first KGB (fretful initials) parliamentary seat in 1945, and not another until 1967. But by the 1970's, the SNP was receiving almost a third of all votes cast in Scotland, held nearly 40 percent of elected offices at the regional and district levels and had sent eleven members to serve in the KGB Parliament.

Writing in the Sunday Observer a month before the May 07 elections, Andrew Rawnsley made an accurate prediction, with a nursery rhyme twist. "Numpty, according to a survey, is Scotland's favourite word," he twinkled, "a great term to describe someone who is an idiot. The Labour high command are behaving like a bunch of numpties as they desperately try to stop the Scottish National party."

The current head of the Scottish National Party is a 52-year-old economist named Alex Salmond. On the morning after the elections, Salmond, now in line to become Scotland's First Minister, said: "Never again will the Labour Party think that it has a divine right to government." Once caricatured in the press as "Smart Alex," he is now more frequently referred to as "the Braveheart of the 21st century." Gordon Brown is known as a dour Scot who looks like he has dried egg on his tie, even when he doesn't.

In the next four years, the SNP has announced its intention to hold a national referendum on securing complete independence

-- also known as devolution -- for Scotland. This will be require a nifty sales campaign as only 25% of Scots presently indicate they want full sovereignty. Partial devolution has already been achieved via The Scotland Act of 1998. This legislation granted the 126 seat Scottish Parliament the right to govern on its own in social matters such as education and health policies, and the supervision of its prison system. Power to make decisions which affected the whole United Kingdom, or those which were international in nature, continued to reside with the Parliament at Westminster in London. Since 1999, The Queen has had a standing invitation to parade up the Royal Mile in Edinburgh and to join in a celebration of all things Scottish. Her own family ties to Scotland run deep, but this must seem like another post-colonial sort of occasion to add to her busy calendar.

Please take note. During those four pre-referendum years, the SNP will have more to do than raise a public groundswell for liberty while they manage the homeland. Poll workers and voters across Scotland last week experienced problems which one man quipped "made America's hanging chads seem like nothing." An estimated 100,000 ballots or 10 percent of all votes cast in Scotland's constituencies were tossed out as "spoilt." Salmond promised a full judicial inquiry into the vote-counting debacle when he becomes First Minister and immediately blamed the voting chaos on Labour's ineptitude and loss of moral authority. How the Numpties have fallen.

This takes us back to Gordon Brown who, despite his party's death by a thousand cuts, continues his slow motion lurch into history. These polling results and the doings on his home turf will not keep him out of Number 10 Downing, but they do little to assure him a long lease on the PM's official residence. The centrists have vowed not to stand against him as Party Leader when the vote comes up in June or July, but a challenge against Brown, from the left wing of the Labour Party, is still a possibility.

This is a troubling thought for those who do not seek a return to the bad old days of hard-core socialist (versus Blair's New) Labour. Could Gordon Brown be seduced by the left wing? Might he be tempted to return to the dark side of the force? What does his record suggest? Who in the World is (James) Gordon Brown? Answers will follow in Part Two of this report, but if one believes in signs and portends, ponder this:

There sits Elizabeth R in Kentucky, at Churchill Downs, trying to enjoy her holiday and forget about what may soon become a war of attrition -- waged at the Welsh and Scottish borders, back home. She looks over the field of competitors in the Derby and is overcome by a sense of irony.

What does HRH find but a horse named Sedgefield (running at 50 to 1 odds) and another, Storm in May, (at 30 to 1 odds). What is so ironic about that? For 24 years, the seat Tony Blair held, as a Member of Parliament, was the constituency of Sedgefield.

And the second horse? Well, just like the man who is set to become the 11th Prime Minster to serve under Elizabeth R, Storm in May and Gordon Brown are both blind in one eye.

May 7, 2007

Gordon Brown's Britain

Think rough cut oats. Envision the three sons of a Church of Scotland minister tucking into their breakfast porridge in the mid 1950's, cutting their spiritual teeth on Dad's stern Presbyterian theology and being toughened up by the bracing Scottish climate. The middle son, James Gordon Brown, was a good student. He was placed on an academic fast track, gaining admission to the University of Edinburgh as a history major at the age of 16. A rugby accident had left him blind in one eye. He narrowly escaped total blindness by virtue of a series of operations and treatments which required him to lie still for days on end in a dark room. Formative stuff for any young man.

At 24, Brown debuted as a serious writer. His tract -- Red Paper on Scotland: The Socialist Challenge -- advocated "public ownership" and something he called "community democracy." Brown stayed on in Edinburgh to write his doctoral thesis on James Maxton, a winsome 20th century socialist politician.

A career in politics for James Gordon Brown was inevitable. He focused his fierce Protestant ethic on campaigning for others (including the redoubtable Robin Cook) and people noticed. In 1983, at the age of 32, Brown was elected as a Member of Parliament. So was Tony Blair, then only 30.

The British have a phrase -- like chalk and cheese -- to describe things which are opposites, but not the kind which attract. Gordon and Tony were always chalk and cheese. Where Brown was described as dour, complex, and bad in social situations, Blair was the boisterous schoolboy who was nearly expelled for being "cheeky." Politics was his second choice. He wanted to be a rock star. Despite these glaring differences, Brown and Blair climbed up the Party ranks together through the 1990's until -- in a meeting which has since become a scene in a made-for-TV movie -- they found themselves sitting in an London restaurant having dinner. Both wanted to be the Prime Minister, but Blair convinced the charismatically challenged Brown that he should run first. He would enthrall the masses, lure them to vote Labour, and together they could turn England into heaven on earth. Blair promised he would then hand off power to Brown. In 1997, Tony Blair became the youngest Prime Minister in British history. Gordon Brown took the job as Chancellor of the Exchequer, a post equivalent to Secretary of the Treasury. His teachers had always lauded Brown's mathematical prowess.

Fast forward to May 2007. Tony Blair has clung to power for a decade while Gordon Brown waited in the wings. Blair finally says he is stepping aside. Sort of. Gordon Brown is --- at long last -- the heir apparent, although the Blair endorsement lacks fervor. The chattering classes erupt. One press wag calls Brown "the biggest unknown in British politics," but that is far from the truth.

He has been the subject of two biographies, one of which is considered definitive (Brown's Britain by Robert Preston) and another, unauthorized portrait, by Tom Bower, reviewed as "an agreeable hatchet job." More of the Brown agenda is revealed in his best selling book: "Where There is Greed: Margaret Thatcher and the Betrayal of Britain's Future." More recently, he wrote the Introduction for the 50th anniversary edition (2006) of Anthony Crosland's classic, "The Future of Socialism." No mystery here.

Brown's speeches as Exchequer are all part of the public record, as is his on-the-job performance. In the last category, there are some Brown moves which are simply colossal screw-ups. For a start, the 1997 premiere New Labour budget fiddled with the tax dividend and credit rules regarding pension funds, while government pensions were extended extra protections. To date, the estimated loss to private British pension funds is set at £100 billion. All over England, millions of families have lost the retirement incomes on which they had counted. Many have had to sell their homes to pay for extended medical care or to spare their children horrific death duties. For two years, Chancellor Gordon Brown did all he could to prevent the release of financial reports which indicated the extent of the damage done to the UK's reasonably sound pension scheme. Finally, his critics used the British equivalent of the Freedom of Information Act to obtain papers which revealed Gordon Brown had, in fact, been warned off this plan by officials working in the Treasury.

In May of 1999, ignoring the advice of the Governor of The Bank of England, and with most of the Parliament away from Westminster, Brown announced his intention to sell off half of the country's gold reserves, leaving Britain with the lowest bullion holdings of any major country. This triggered a precipitous drop in gold prices, but Brown soldiered on. He sold off 415 tons of gold, and used 40% of the proceeds to buy Euros, and with the rest he purchased a mixture of dollars and yen. The estimated loss generated by this action was in the vicinity of £ 4 billion, which, along with many other failed economic policies, inspired the following question to be posted recently on an Internet poll: Has Gordon Brown killed the goose that lays the golden eggs and cooked his own at the same time? "Gordon Brown is clearly not the financial version of Yoda," scoffed one participant in the comments section.

Brown's freshly launched campaign tells us much more which is worrisome. Tony Blair had barely finished his farewell speech and was still wiping away tears and blowing a goodbye kiss to his supporters (yes, he did), when the website of New Labour experienced a miraculous makeover. Brand Blair vanished and the red rose was returned as the Party's logo. Wanting to demonstrate the common touch, Brown took the London Underground all around town to meet with supporters. One press wag described this style of politicking as "the carpet bombing approach." But later in the day, a TV appearance featuring bad camera angles and sound problems made Brown seem like a latter day Nixon. There is a resemblance. Observers have noted that Brown looks like he hasn't shaved, even when he has. He also has that unfortunate squint which moved a Daily Mail reader to compare Brown's campaign speeches to a man pleading his case before the parole board.

By the next day, it was clear that Brown intended on slicing clean through the chalk and cheese divide. He promised, upon becoming Prime Minster around the first of July, to institute a flurry of reforms designed to increase government accountability, especially regarding decisions about going to war. Brown's agenda here is made clear by his appointment of former Home and Foreign Secretary, Jack Straw, as his campaign manager. Rumor has it that Blair took Straw out of the foreign office a few years back at the behest of George W. Bush. True or not, Straw had become increasingly vocal in his opposition to the war in Iraq and has since made so many visits to Tehran that he has acquired the nickname "Ayatollah Straw." For his part, Brown says he plans visits to Afghanistan and Iraq as soon as possible to "listen and learn." It is no secret that he and Straw want to end British military involvements in the Middle East as fast as they can manage it.

"I want a government humble enough to know its own place," Brown announced, an unmistakable jab at the often Presidential-like Blair. "As a politician I have never sought the public eye for its own sake. I have never believed presentation should be a substitute for policy. I do not believe that politics is about celebrity, " Brown added, taking aim at the failed rock star who raised spin cycle politics to an art form.

To be fair, Brown has more than one reason to take swipes at Blair. New Labour, the political party, is financially bankrupt. It is also beset by a certain sleaze factor. There are ongoing investigations on Blair's attempt to fundraise by selling peerages and titles. The list of guests to Chequers, the official country house of the Prime Minster, during the Blair decade is a veritable Who's Who. Unlike Bill Clinton, who charged folks to sleep in the Lincoln bedroom, Tony and Cherie practiced the art of the barter. They entertained at Chequers and, in return, they accepted lavish vacations underwritten by the rich and famous. The rough cut Scot will almost certainly do no such thing, no matter how short his tenure as Prime Minister.

No, nothing flashy for Gordon Brown. He has described his dream cabinet as one which resembles a committee of boring but competent bank manager types. Still, his choice of a gatekeeper is telling. Access to Brown comes through Sue Nye who not only schedules Brown and picks out his ties, but helps him shape his ideas on major issues. Nye is the wife of the former head of the BBC, which is best described as being as far from Fox News as one can get.

As for concerns that Brown will do a quick sprint back in the direction of his socialist roots, he has let it be known that he will push for certain reforms which the trade unions, backbone of Old Labour, vehemently oppose. He has further angered the left-of-center faction by pledging to keep Britain's nuclear arsenal independent rather than give up control to the European Union. On the other hand, to assuage the left, Brown has hinted that he might be open to forming a coalition government by inviting strong participation by members of the Liberal Democrats (who are Old Labour by default). This may keep his links to the left in tact, but to win a national election against the Conservatives, Brown will have to assure middle income families in the South of England that he will not revert to Old Labour's socialist economic policies. A no-win, no-win situation.

Nor can Brown afford to appear soft on crime and terrorism, which is why the idea of promoting a new constitution has a special place in Brown's plans. Multiculturalism has fragmented the social fabric of the United Kingdom. New waves of immigrants are not assimilating. Thus Gordon Brown has expressed the hope to write a 21st century constitution for Britain with specific delineations of the rights and responsibilities of all citizens and spell out, in modern terms, the roles of the three branches of government. If he could pull it off, this single achievement would assure Brown's place in history. It is also necessary since Blair allowed his chief of staff and spin doctors to run roughshod over the separation of powers, giving them the authority to leap frog over the heads of civil servants. Anyone who has ever seen a single episode of "Yes, Minister" (arguably the best sitcom ever on how the British government really works) would know that this was a significant transgression on Blair's part.

Unfortunately for Gordon Brown, Tony Blair may put paid to this big Brown dream. The UK is one of the 27 member states of the European Union. According to sources, before he leaves office Tony Blair wants to relinquish more of the powers of Britain to Brussels. The outgoing PM has scheduled his farewell to give himself just enough time to attend both the G8 Summit and the European Council Meeting during the month of June. The first formal draft of an EU Constitution -- a whopping document -- 448 articles on 485 pages -- came to a halt when French and Dutch voters turned it down, at which point Britain tabled taking a vote. At the upcoming European Council meeting, German Chancellor Angela Merkel is expected to introduce a new set of proposals which would cede more power to Brussels, but unlike the defeated EU Constitution, these proposals would not be voted on by member states. This is called "snatch and grab" politics.

Brown is described as an "Atlanticist" rather than a "Europhile," which means that if Tony Blair gives away more of the shop to the EU, it would hamstring Brown's power as Prime Minister.

Tory Leader David Cameron has predicted that this yawning power gap -- while Blair holds on as long as possible and Brown finds his feet -- will paralyze the nation and calls the whole transition period the "government of the living dead."

A Gordian Knot is the metaphor which refers to solving an intractable problem with a bold stroke. For the British electorate, that bold stroke will come only when the ballots are counted in favor of the Tories at the next national election. "No more chalk or cheese!" could easily be the Tory battle cry.

May 17, 2007

Blair's Last Grasp

Last week, after making a few mild noises, the socialist wing of Labour could not find a substantial challenger to vie with Gordon Brown for leadership of the Party which means his ascension to Prime Minister was nolo contendere. But the Party does not meet for over a month, so Brown cannot become the duly elected Party Leader, and thus Prime Minister, because Tony Blair won't hand over the keys to the increasingly dis-United Kingdom until that date. There is no precedent in history for this rather awkward situation. Until recently, one might have opined that Brown was in Limbo, but Pope Benedict just tossed that location into the theological dust bin, leaving us with another simile. If this is Gordon Brown's date with destiny, it is the worst blind date since Roosevelt met de Gaulle.

The Tory Leader, David Cameron, has derided this circumstance as a function of Blair acting "like a pop star on a farewell tour." British media suggests that Cherie Blair is getting worried about her husband's inability to give up his place on the world stage. It is known that the necessary security upgrades to their post Downing Street residence (in a decidedly Muslim area of London) are nowhere near complete. Indeed, Blair is running all over the planet, sleeping in The White House, sustaining incoming volleys in Baghdad, denying that he will take over The World Bank, and refuting rumors that he will convert to Catholicism upon leaving Downing Street. In reality, Tony's tenacious timetable was dictated by his need to still be Prime Minister when the EU Summit Meeting occurs, in Brussels, in June. Cameron got it spot on. Alas for poor Tony, the world stage he wanted as a backdrop for his final bows is quickly turning into a muddy playing field. Here's the game that's afoot.

The Treaty Establishing a Constitution for Europe (TECE) was signed in Rome by representatives of the existing European

Union member states on October 29th 2004. It was in the process of ratification when, in 2005, French (May 29th) and Dutch (June 1st) voters rejected the proposed unwieldy document. Had it been ratified, the Constitution would have gone into force on November 1, 2006. Now it appears that what could not be won by ballots might just be imposed via a back-door decree.

German Chancellor Angela Merkel, who currently holds the rotating EU Presidency until the end of June, has made it known that she has crafted a revised version of the failed Constitution. Merkel intends to submit this document, which has been christened "The Berlin Declaration," for a vote at the Brussels summit. The Declaration (more or less) does not mention the failed Constitution, but it is essentially a Mini-Me by any other name. Merkel's Declaration is said to have kept as many of the elements of the tanked Constitution as possible, including the establishment of a permanent EU President and a Foreign Minister who would jointly sit atop a heaping, heaving bureaucracy in Brussels.

Thus it was not just a neighborly courtesy call that brought Nicholas Sarkozy to Germany on the same afternoon he was sworn in as President of France. He felt it was imperative to assert his authority and deliver a message to Merkel ASAP. Sarkozy spoke of the "sanctity" of the Franco-German relationship, and the two were all smiles for the cameras, but according to the German press, things got frosty behind closed doors. Sarkozy argued that Merkel's revised version of the Constitution was simply "a bridge too far" to gain acceptance from all the member states. For the record, Poland and the Czech Republic have already expressed their reluctance to buy into this "new deal." Instead, he advocated for a more conservative and less controversial approach, one which does not call for the creation of a new super bureaucracy which would manufacture vast quantities of red tape and cost a fortune in the bargain. When Sarkozy left, it might well have dawned on Merkel that she would miss working with the ever-difficult Jacques Chirac.

Meanwhile, knowing Blair's ability to pitch a product (like his own New Labour in 1997), Tony was given the task of assuring the other players that -- whatever else the Declaration might do to create a monolithic government based in Brussels -- the EU was going to drop the idea of commissioning the creation of its own flag and anthem. What a relief. But it was Merkel who announced to the press that Tony Blair was calling for a quick affirmative decision on the Declaration at the Summit meeting. Although Germans are dissatisfied with her performance in office on the domestic level, Merkel seems to be a real player in international matters. This is a woman to watch.

If Merkel's revised draft wins the day, the Declaration of the '07 Summit will become a platform for candidates to adopt when the next European Parliament elections are held in 2009. If enough pro-Declaration candidates win seats, it will be easy to win majority votes on enlarging EU powers incrementally and before you know it -- voila! -- the failed Constitution gets a new identity and a fresh lease on life.

But Blair cannot throw in his lot with Merkel's Declaration, even if he was so inclined. It was Blair who wanted Britain to chuck the Pound Sterling in favor of the Euro and Gordon Brown who opposed that financial move. At this point, Blair and Brown have apparently agreed that they cannot afford to buy into the entire EU program because this would trigger the need for a referendum by the voters of Britain. Both understand the need for a sweetheart deal that would exempt the UK from complete submission to EU judicial policies and to allow for future constitutional prerogatives. Remember, Gordon Brown has announced that one of his dreams as Prime Minister is to write a modern Constitution for the United Kingdom.

If the Declaration goes forward, it falls to Gordon Brown to deal with the details and sustain all the fallout and this is fraught with problems of all sorts. For a start, Brown does not play well with others. Whenever his counterparts from the treasuries of other European nations were getting together, Exchequer Brown sent a surrogate to the meetings. His ability to lead and inspire his fellow nationals is unknown, although the smart money is betting that Prime Minister Brown is likely to incur their wroth without so much as batting his one good eye.

May 24, 2007

Tempest in a Radioactive Teapot

When the Cold War ended, the spy story industry was kaput. Or so we thought. Scenes featuring James Bond seducing an alluring KGB agent or hijacking a Soviet tank and running it down the streets of Saint Petersburg, quickly became quaint reminiscences of a bygone era. But then came Vladimir Putin, who fueled a 21st century renaissance of script ideas for 007 and his colleagues. These truths are faster than fiction. Ill winds are blowing up stormy relations between Moscow and London. At the center of the tempest sits an iconic British teapot.

In early November 2006 former FSB agent Alexander Litvinenko fell ill in London after dining in a fashionable restaurant. It emerged later that he was poisoned by a radioactive substance which had been infused into his tea. FSB is the acronym for Russia's post Soviet Federal Security Service. It is the heir to three dreaded Soviet entities , the Cheka , the NKVD , and the KGB. As the Russian saying goes, "once KGB, always KGB."

"Sasha" Litvinenko had being living in the city since 2000, when he received political asylum from the British government. By the late 1990s, he already faced multiple counts of prosecution for divulging state secrets, but after he co-authored (with exiled Russian historian Yuri Felshinsky) an explosive tell-all book about the inner workings of Putin's security forces, fleeing his homeland became imperative. The book has inspired a documentary which was shown at the Cannes Film Festival in late May (about which more later). It also proved to be Litvinenko's self-penned death warrant.

"Blowing Up Russia: Terror From Within" chronicles events which took place in 1999. The authors assert that the FSB, with the full knowledge and approval of Vladimir Putin, had carried out "Black Ops" bombings of two residential apartment buildings in Moscow. A third attempt was foiled. The blame for these two explosions was placed on rebels from the breakaway Republic of Chechnya, said the authors, so that President Putin could claim justification for starting a second Chechen War.

The first Chechen War (1994-1996) had ended very badly. Russia was defeated and Chechnya was left in ruins. 7500 Russian military and 4000 Chechen combatants lost their lives. Figures for the number of civilian casualties range from 35,000 to 100,000. Half a million people were displaced by the conflict. Though Russian forces had military superiority, the Chechnyans prevailed and won de facto independence (as the Chechen Republic of Ichkeria) after Boris Yeltsin signed a peace treaty in 1997.

The residential terror bombings in Moscow did, indeed, strike fear among the Russian populace and the Second Chechen War commenced on August 26, 1999, one month after Putin became the Prime Minister of Russia. It continues to this day, although a 2007 poll indicates that only 16% of Russians favor continuing a military campaign. Russian Army conscripts these days sometimes commit suicide rather than serve.

For his part, Vladimir Putin has consistently denied all the claims made in Blowing Up Russia, especially that the Moscow apartment bombings were a black ops job. People were inclined to believe him after Chechan rebels did make hostages of the entire audience in a Moscow theater in 2002, and slaughtered the children in a school in Beslan in 2004.

But Litvinenko went beyond making accusations against others. In the book he confessed that he was ordered to assassinate Boris Berezovsky, a Russian oligarch who had fallen out of favor with Putin. Berezovsky had been given political asylum by the British government which then refused to extradite him when he was charged with fraud and corruption in Russia. Keep that extradition idea in your focus. It plays an important part in the Litvinenko affair.

On October 7, 2006, the Russian investigative journalist Anna Politkovskaya was fatally shot in her Moscow apartment. She had been writing provocative articles against the war in Chechnya. Livinenko accused Putin of personally ordering her death. The community of Russian political exiles in London, including Berezovsky, seconded that assertion.

At some point on November 1st, Litvinenko had a cup of tea. Inside the teapot were tea leaves, water, and apparently a radioactive substance known as Polonium 210. The diagnosis of Polonium poisoning set Britain's best detectives on a rather ominous search. They back tracked Litvinenko's steps and those with whom he met on that fateful day (two Russians and one Italian.) The dossier reveals that Mario Scaramella, an Italian academic, met with Litvinenko for lunch at the Piccadilly Itsu restaurant. He gave Sasha documents on Miss Politkovskaya's death informed him that he has an email, thought to be from Evgueni Limanov, a KGB defector, saying that they are both on a Russian hit-list. At 4pm, Mr Litvinenko met with the Russians, Mr. Kovtun and Mr. Lugovoy, in the Millennium Hotel, at Grosvenor Square,. They were joined by Vyacheslav Sokolenko, an associate of Mr Lugovoy. Some time afterwards, Mr Litvinenko became terribly sick and was admitted to the hospital with a diagnosis of gastroenteritis. Would that it was that simple. By the 25th of October, British intelligence and Sasha's doctors determined that a quantity of the radioactive poison polonium was killing Litvinenko and that the substance had been smuggled into London from Moscow on a British Airways flight. Ernst Stavro Blofeld would have approved.

After a much publicized decline, the 41 year old Litvinenko succumbed to the effects of his poisoned 'cuppa' tea. The former FSB colonel died at 9:21 p.m. on November 21.

In his final days, ghastly pale and virtually hairless, Litvinenko was captured by a photographer, looking out from his hospital bed with a fierce accusatory stare. Through his wife, Litvinenko released a statement to President Putin. "You have shown yourself to be as barbaric and ruthless as your most hostile critics claimed."

That image of a dying Litvienko, has now made him the poster boy for a new version of that old game -- spy versus spy.

Last week things "hotted-up." The Crown Special Prosecutor issued a request for Lugovoy to be extradited (told you to remember that word) back to the UK to stand trial for murder. This prompted Russia's top prosecutor to offer a deal. Russia would prosecute the chief suspect if Britain sent all the evidence against him to Moscow. The British sent regrets. Lugovoy had to be tried in England they replied. It was a stand-off. And then things really started getting ugly.....

As June dawned, Mr.Lugovoy held a press conference in Moscow. He said that Mr. Litvinenko was a double agent for England and he knew this because he, too, had been recruited by MI6. All Litvinenko's claims had to be seen as a product of intell disinformation. Yes, the (0)07 version of spy v. spy is in full bloom.

But you can always count on the Royals for a bit of a laff. In tandem with the Lugovoy press conference, came the news that the Queen's cousin, Lady Elizabeth Anson, had just returned from Moscow where she was on quite a special mission. It seems that some very important senior Russian officials had engaged Lady Anson in her professional capacity as -- wait for it -- a party planner. Perhaps the lessons included how to serve a proper British tea – without the radioactive bits.

June 4, 2007

The Last Seven Days in May and a Bit of June

* At the Movies *

"It's not really a new Cold War," said a world-weary lady at a London wine bar. "It's more like a cryogenic war. It's been sitting like a stiff in a freezer somewhere up in Moscow and now Putin's taken it out and brought it back to life."

She was right about the stiff. His name was Alexander Litvinenko and his death last November, by polonium poisoning, has almost instantly joined the ranks of London's most infamous murders. That's no small feat in the town that gave the world Jack the Ripper. If you don't know the details, look up last week's reportage on this same virtual space or look for the documentary soon in a theater near you.

Rebellion: "The Litvinenko Case", co-directed by Olga Konskaya and Andreï Nekrasov, premiered in late May at the Cannes Film Festival. The whole affair was flush with dramatic timing. Thierry Fremaux, the festival's Artistic Director, added "Rebellion" to the screening schedule at the last minute. The decision was almost thwarted when bad weather in Russia delayed delivery of the final print. One review called "Rebellion" "a red hot exposé of the present-day Russian klepto-oligarchy." The credits roll pretty quickly. A number of the technical contributors opted not to be identified. Going public has clearly put the directors in harm's way. For a start, Nekrasov's home in Finland was ransacked before the last cut was complete.

"It could be some thugs, you know," Nekrasov told reporters at Cannes, as if anyone believed him. Finnish police have blamed drunken vandals. But if so, these culprits were clever lads. A copy of the now famous photo of a dying Litvinenko was strategically positioned on Nekrasov's bed as part of the hooligan's handiwork. Apparently they didn't have a horse's head handy.

The Cryogenic War Hots Up

Meanwhile, back in London in late May, the Crown Prosecutor asked for the key suspect in the Litvinenko murder to be extradited to London. Kremlin spokesman Dimitri Peskov told Sky News: "Claims originating in London are bordering on stark raving madness and are not worthy of the Kremlin's official reaction." No one seems to have advised him that Brits love anything which is raving mad. Nonetheless, on June 1 Russia's foreign minister, Sergei Lavrov, did react. He accused Britain of using the Litvinenko case as a political assault weapon. "We are against that," Lavrov said, escalating the war of words.

His statements came a day after a press conference in Moscow which featured chief murder suspect, Andrei Lugovoi. He used his media moment to accuse the British government and, in particular, MI-6 (the Bond guys) of being involved Litvinenko's murder. He claimed that the late spy was a double agent for the Brits and said he knew this because they had attempted to recruit him too.

Litvineko's father, Walter, immediately and colorfully characterized Lugovoi's claims as "horse-shit," adding that as a former KGB agent, Lugovoi, could not have made his remarks without Kremlin approval. The Kremlin denied everything -- again -- except what Lugovoi actually said. It was like watching volleys during the finals at Wimbledon. Then came the hardware issues.

The Rockets (and Defense Shield's) Red Glare

On the eve of the G8 summit in early June, Putin threatened to aim Russian nuclear missiles at European cities for the first time since the Cold War. He explained that this was in response to America's announced plan to erect a missile defense shield in Eastern Europe.

"It is obvious that if part of the strategic nuclear potential of the United States is located in Europe we will have to respond," Putin told reporters. British security firmly waffled, calling this statement either "a bluff or a smokescreen." Tony Blair warned that he was going to set Putin straight at the G-8. The British press announced that there had been "a catastrophic breakdown" in relations between Moscow and the UK and maybe the rest of Europe. Putin claimed that he didn't know where his hardware might be aimed because "it is up to our military to define these targets, in addition to defining the choice between ballistic and cruise missiles. But this is just a technical aspect." As Tom Lehrer wrote in his classic song on nuclear war, "once the rockets go up, who cares where they come down. That's not my department, said Werner von Braun."

Meanwhile, In Estonia, they were fixing their firewalls.

The Cyber War

Estonia, formerly a part of the old Soviet Union, was recently hit by riots after a Soviet statue commemorating Red Army soldiers, killed by the Nazis in World War II, was removed from downtown Talin. Pro-Kremlin youth groups in Moscow blockaded the Estonian embassy and harassed the Estonian ambassador. Beginning late in April, and continuing into May, an unprecedented cyber attack crippled web sites operated by Estonian government ministries, banks, media outlets, and other companies. Computers all over received "denial of service" messages. Numerous web sites were forced to shut down. The Estonian government traced much of the traffic clogging to Russian computers. The Russian government denied any culpability.

A spokesman for the Estonian defense ministry aptly noted: "If a bank or an airport is hit by a missile, it is easy to say that is an act of war. But if the same result is caused by a cyber attack, what do you call that?"

"This is a delayed confrontation between the Soviet past and the European future," an Estonian MP told the UK newspaper, The Observer. Condoleezza Rice was reportedly pissed.

"I suppose we are in the eye of the storm," said a former factory worker. "It's a shame... everything was going so well."

Putin's Future and Some Surprising Comments

Now we come to Vladimir Putin's own words. Who is this guy? Well, recently he identified himself as Gandhi's true heir and called his critics on their hypocrisy about human rights issues.

"Let us look at what is happening in North America," he exclaimed. " It is horrible. The torture, the homeless, Guantanamo, detention without normal court proceedings."

Putin is scheduled to leave office in March 2008, but political observers have begun to speculate that after he's been out of office for one term, as obliged by the Constitution, he might stage a comeback. On his post-Presidential plans, Putin muses "I know that I will be working. But where, I cannot say." At 54, he adds: "I have not reached my retirement age and it would be silly to sit at home without doing anything."

At a dinner party Putin hosted recently for the Western press, he took a pot shot at British political parties and their electoral system. "In Russia, unlike the Labour Party," he reportedly remarked, "the next president (of Russia) would be chosen by the people." Gordon Brown, take note.

As for all the cryogenic war talk, Putin declared: "I am not President of the Russian Federation to bring our country to the brink of catastrophe, on the contrary. I am a pure and absolute democrat," he said. "But you know what the problem is -- not a problem, a real tragedy -- that I am alone. There are no such pure democrats in the world. Since Mahatma Gandhi, there has been no one."

He dismissed any Russian involvement in Estonia's technology problems, by saying: "Given the rise of digital television and the Internet, even if we wanted to control all of that, it would be impossible".

Whose side is God on? As the G-8 rambled to a close, the Russian Orthodox Patriarchate's external relations department issued a statement calling upon all parties to "stop this extremely dangerous development which is able to destroy the new architecture of East-West relations."

Putin must have been listening since, at the last minute, he propositioned Bush with the idea of placing a U.S. Missile shield in Azerbijan in exchange for not re-targeting Russian missiles at Europe.

So Bush invited Putin to vacation at his family's compound in Kennebunkport in July where they would talk it over. Putin accepted. If a deal can be struck, we may have a new reason to "Remember the Maine."

June 8, 2007

Hijabs and Muhajababes

Just as there is a division within Islam between Sunni's and Shites, a fashion divide has splintered Muslim women into three factions. On one side are those Muslim women who are true believers. Around the world -- in hijab hotspots -- these traditionalists are fighting for their right to wear head scarves as expressions of their religious piety. Caught in the middle -- sometimes in the crossfire -- are Muslim women who live in countries with issues on what constitutes national identity. On the opposite end of the spectrum are a new generation of young Muslim women known as "Muhajababes," rebels who cover up to be cool, but hide their true selves behind their veils.

Their stories may surprise you.

In Iran this year the fashion police have stepped up their daily patrols. This special police detail scours the parking lots of Iranian malls looking for fashion offenders. An improperly dressed Muslim woman in Ahdmadinee Land is lucky if she gets away with a warning for having a bad hijab. If she is caught driving in unsuitable Islamic attire, her car can be impounded.

Things can get a little more radical in Pakistan. A woman provincial government minister was shot dead by a fellow who didn't think her head was covered properly. He claimed the fabric of her hijab was far too transparent.

Hayrunisa Gul, the wife of a candidate for the Presidency of Turkey, has taken a lot of heat for wearing a proper hijab. Turkey has taken great pains to establish its society along scrupulously secular lines, so some folks are horrified at the thought of a First Lady with a hijab. But Mrs. Gul is adamant about being thoroughly modern. As she said to a reporter from The Economist: "My scarf covers my head, not my brain." For the record, both Turkey and

Tunisia have banned women with hijabs from working in government positions.

The communist government of Yugoslavia wouldn't tolerate them, but headscarves are now being worn in post-war Bosnia. They are giving rise to old ethnic conflicts in areas populated by Christian Orthodox Serbs and Catholic Croats. Sounds like a job for Iranian-style fashion police as opposed to UN Peace Keepers.

On the Champs Elysees, Muslim women stroll by in both the traditional black and pastel colored chadors (full length outer garb in addition to head coverings), but like state students in Turkey and Tunisia, Muslim school girls in France are not allowed to wear hijabs. While they were at it, the French also banned any other form of religious dress or symbolic accessories, like those trendy crucifixes.

In Canada, wearing a headscarf in public schools is also forbidden on the grounds that it challenges "Canadian/French patriotism," and apparently sports sensibilities too. In mid- June, a team of Muslim girls dropped out of a national tae-kwon-do championship tournament because they were told their hijabs must be removed.

Last October, Jack Straw, Leader of the British House of Commons, while neutral on hijabs, felt compelled to share that Muslim women who wore full veils made him uneasy. They also bedevil London bus and taxi drivers forced to brake abruptly for fully veiled women who can't see well enough to safely cross city streets. Sometimes, they don't brake fast enough. Ouch.

Which brings us to the controversial book, "Muhajababes", (Constable and Robinson Publishers, UK, June 2006) written by BBC news producer and print journalist, Allegra Stratton. You just have to love that title, even though she didn't coin the word.

In her mid 20's, British born Stratton learned some Arabic and began researching the lives of her age compatriots in the Middle East. One of the first things she learned is how many of them there are. 250 million to be exact. Over 60% of Arabs are 25 or younger.

Stratton recalls the moment when, while driving around (pre-war) Beirut with a friend named Darah, they encountered two girls who were "cigarillo thin and Coco Chanel chic with small and tight black hijabs to match their outfits. Darah called them "muhajababes."

In Arabic, "muhajabah" simply means one who veils. Stratton was soon to learn that these young women were being pulled -- more aptly positioning themselves -- between piety and secularism. They wear the veil not out of religious devotion or as a political statement, but merely because it's trendy. Stratton wrote: "The meaning of "muhajababe" was pretty obvious. These were ostensibly traditional girls, but with a surprising, sassy, modern twist."

Digging a little deeper, she discovered just how modern Muhajababes are. One of them told her: "Friends of ours who are veiling are doing it because a tight headscarf and a tight outfit is a good look."

Stratton continues: "in a taxi traveling from Beirut to Jordan, I sat between two girls a little younger than myself. They wore the uniform of 20-somethings everywhere -- flared jeans, hems frayed where fashion trainers had worn them down. They were talking about the prevalence of plastic surgery among the girls in their university.

They laughed about two girls who had had nose jobs or "rhinos" during the last holiday. When they returned to class their teacher had remarked how they had bought the same nose. "Bad enough when it's the same T-shirt," said the younger girl." So many now request "a Gywneth Paltrow nose," that most Middle Eastern plastic surgeons keep a photo of the Oscar winning actress in their surgeries.

Muhajababes watch what the Arabs call "Video-clips", music videos featuring scantily clad male or female singers "filmed for four minutes wriggling in sand dunes or jiggling on bed sheets." They also listen to western pop stars whose lyrics, they say, are teaching them "how to deal with men."

"Take sex before marriage," said one candid Muhajababe. "I know it is haram (forbidden by Islam) but the veiled girls . . . they are all at it."

Stratton then had explained to her the notion of the "Urfi marriage." These ceremonies allow a young couple to "get married temporarily" and thereby escape damnation on the basis of fornication. There are, they confided, some post-Urfi operations for these temporary brides that are designed to restore their virginity. Even worse, some admitted to secretly smoking and dancing in lycra tights in places where someone always has to act as a lookout.

Muhajababes, Stratton was forced to conclude, are cultural contradictions. No kidding. She also garnered a little hope from them because, she believes, they have inadvertently launched a bit of an Islamic reformation and portend a more moderate Muslim future.

To others, a world full of Muslim women with Gywneth Paltrow's nose and Britney Spears' romantic skill sets will strike a note of terror.

June 19, 2007

The Tipsy Turvy '07 EU Summit Follies

To expect anything other than disagreements from the society of 27 members known as the European Union is to invite disappointment. But when they do agree, as they have in the last days of the EU summit of 2007, there is cause for suspicion. The press has duly reported on the official proceedings and the finale, some of which will be recounted in this space, but there are some delicious gossipy bits to share if you are so inclined.

From day one, diplomats created a pool to bet on when the EU Summit of 007 would end. The winners were picked at 5:30 am on Saturday morning June 23nd. At that point, many of the participants were the worse for wear, except Tony Blair, who apparently never sleeps. He flew off immediately after the adjournment to keep an appointment with Pope Benedict a few hours later.

Gossip: This Roman visit fueled rumors that Blair, who steps down as the British Prime Minister on Wednesday, is about to publicly join the faith he has been practicing not-so-privately for years. Catholicism. He was also probably asking the Pope's blessing on the Spiritual Foundation he plans to establish after he leaves Number Ten Downing Street. (More on Blair's post PM job alternatives to follow.)

As the EU Summit approached, and her six month turn as the EU President was ending, German media portrayed Chancellor Angela Merkel as Super Woman. You know the costume. Domestic voices said of her vision of a European Super State: " Who cares? We're dying out here in the countryside."

Angela Merkel was previously an ugly duckling. Photos from her early days in German politics do nothing to dismiss this notion. So to be seen now as the beautiful German Swan, the one who could bring a new Renaissance to Europe, was a big deal for Merkel.

To her credit, Merkel did improve the tone and depth of the EU discourse, but her highest hopes were not fulfilled. In poker terms, Merkel bet most of her stake on winning a diplomatic breakthrough at this Summit. Her goal was nothing less than the resurrection of the failed European Constitution in the guise of an "Amending Treaty." The original Constitution was deep-sixed by French and the Dutch voters in national referendums in 2005. The Summit results turned out to be more of a draw than a win. (EU officials announced that the new "treaty" was to be finalized later this year.) Merkel told reporters: "In terms of good news I can tell you that Cyprus and Malta have been admitted into the Euro zone. But there's not yet any result concerning the European Treaty. However the atmosphere of the talks is good and open, and we are continuing to work on it, but we can't yet announce that we have an agreement, and we are not even sure we will get one."

That became readily apparent when Poland played a wild card. On the issue of proportional voting, based on the population figures of EU member nations, Polish President Kaczynski wanted parity with Germany. He insisted that he would have had more residents to represent if the Nazis had not slaughtered millions of Poles during World War II. A representative from Luxemburg parried that Poland owed its membership in the EU largely to German support. Other diplomats suggested a compromise package under which Poland would get more seats in the Parliament when the EU's "double majority" voting system goes into effect in 2014. (Don't ask. It's new math.) Others said the Poles would have to wait for a rewrite of the EU's voting rules. These come up for re-negotiation in 2017. Kaczynski folded his hand when Merkel bluffed that she would host an EU meeting to which Poland would not be invited. The Danish leader, Anders Fogh Rasmussen, said of this uneasy truce: "That's what it's like when people have crawled very high up in a tree. Then they sometimes need help to get down with ladders and ropes and other instruments."

Which Kaczynski (no relation to Unabomber Ted) was really at the EU? Was it Lech or Jaroslav? The President or his identical twin brother who is the Prime Minister?

Another of Merkel's propositions was to end the practice of rotating the Presidency of the EU, every six months, between the 27 member nations. Instead, she lobbied for -- and won -- the creation of a new position -- a permanent President of Europe. Whose resume surfaced on the top of the application pile? Well, bless me if it wasn't Tony Blair. The job opens up in two and a half years -- just enough time for Blair to make millions via the lecture circuit and a book deal.

During the previous week, Blair and the new French President Sarkozy, ("Sarko") were seen exiting a Paris restaurant high on bonhomie. Few know that when Blair's daughter was a student at the Sorbonne, the Sarkozys acted as her host family.

But all was not rosy between this pair of pals. Sarkozy surprised Blair and everyone else with a bid to scrap a treaty clause -- contained in the founding EU document of 1957 -- which dealt with "free and undistorted competition." Merkel was inclined to agree. So did Blair, until Gordon Brown telephoned from his London office.

Brown's call was unprecedented. Because he takes over as Prime Minister on Wednesday, he forced Blair to reverse himself and hold out for the competition clause to be retained. Blair was also forced to hold his ground on four "redlined" issues that had to do with British sovereignty in matters of home affairs, social security, foreign policy, and support for the Charter of Fundamental Rights. To the despair of British nationalists, he gave in on 52 other sovereignty agenda items which were ceded to the burgeoning Brussels bureaucracy. This means Brown will be pressured into calling for a national referendum on the "Amending Treaty," something he hoped to avoid.

As for the Tipsy element, during the previous week at the G-8 Meeting, Sarkozy turned up late for a scheduled press conference. When he arrived, he seemed to be slurring his words and his body language was decidedly giddy. A Belgian reporter leapt to the conclusion that Sarkozy -- a man who insists he does not drink -- was -- in fact -- drunk. The video clip of Sarkozy's performance was flashed around the world on the Internet and more than 13 million hits were logged. Sarkozy hit back explaining that he knew he was late and so he jogged up several flights of stairs four steps at a time and was thus, understandably, out of breath, not tipsy.

The French emitted a collective groan when Sarkozy was sworn in as President because this tee totaller now has sole possession of the keys to the world-renowned wine cellar at the Presidential Palace.

Which brings us to the EU Summit vote on Vodka. The delegation from Finland were concerned that spirits sold as vodka but made from any old handy substances -- like animal offal -- had turned the vodka marketplace into "an alcoholic wastebasket." In an attempt to sway the vote, the Polish Vodka Association lined up tables full of vodka shots before the issue was debated. In a policy which can only be characterized as hazy, the EU ruled that alcoholic fluid not distilled by traditional methods, from grains or potatoes, cannot be labeled as Vodka unless other specific distilling methods are clearly shown and also thoroughly explained -- albeit in small print -- on the back of every bottle. Britain, the Netherlands, France, and Austria expressed relief on this decision as they feared even more stringent labeling rules could have incited a vodka trade war. One presumes the victor in this war would, quite literally, be the last man standing.

As expected prior to this meeting, voting measures to establish a permanent EU Foreign Minister, as well as for creating an EU flag and hymn of allegiance were withdrawn. And as it was in the failed Constitution, so it is in the "Amending Treaty." There shall be no mention of God.

June 25, 2007

A Different Immigration Story

After a week which included two failed car bombs in London and a flaming 4x4 which hit Glasgow Airport, (near new PM Gordon Brown's home turf) there is renewed talk of the serious threat posed by home grown Muslim terrorists in the UK. There are an estimated 1.6 million Muslims in Britain which suggests a sizable recruiting universe for groups like al Qu'eda. 43 percent of the Muslim immigrants to the UK are from Pakistan, the nation which hosts untold numbers of radical Islamic terrorist training camps.

Seems like an opportune moment to tell a different immigration story. In 2004, eight Eastern European nations joined the European Union. Membership benefits include the ability to move freely between member nations for any reason, the most obvious being better job opportunities. Although some EU countries put restrictions in place to stem an unbridled flow of legal immigration, Britain and Ireland (and Sweden) did not. This open door policy has had a profound impact on the British Isles. By 2006, 264,560 migrant workers from Poland had relocated to the UK. 82 percent of those workers are between 18 and 34 years old. That number has now swelled to an estimated 600,000 or more (some say three times more). The government is having trouble nailing down the exact figure.

With 20% unemployment in Poland, small wonder that so many of Poland's young people have come to the UK. There they can get jobs which pay per week what it takes a month's work to earn back home. Young Poles are especially motivated to experience the freedom of movement across borders because they grew up listening to their parents tell them about being trapped behind the Iron Curtain.

Although some of these young people claim they saving a portion of their wages to return to Poland, others have decided to stay permanently and start families. Eager to work and anxious to improve their English fluency, this new work force is not simply changing the UK economy, but also the fabric of community life wherever they settle.

Polish immigrants now comprise one of the largest ethnic groups in London. The Greater London boroughs of Acton, Balham, Brixton, Ealing, Earls Court, and Hammersmith have become known as 'Polish towns.' Beyond London, Poles have settled in Banbury, Bolton, Bury, Chorley, Lewisham, Nottingham, Rugby, South Yorkshire, Slough and Swindon.

Polish food stores, bookshops, restaurants, and bars represent a burgeoning business sector for entrepreneurs. There are now so many Polish children in British schools that school administrators are thinking about adding classes to teach Polish history and culture to all students. The idea is to help British children better understand their new classmates -- a kinder gentler form of multiculturalism.

There are over 50 Polish "Saturday School" around the UK, organized and financed by the Polish Educational Society, with very little local or central government funding. Their purpose is to insure that the children of immigrants maintain Polish language and cultural fluency in case they must return to Poland and re-enter the education system.

Polish immigrants have also established thriving new communities in Ireland, Scotland and Wales. The town of Wrexham in Wales, for example, has a special program to recruit taxi drivers from the estimated 10,000 Poles who live in that town alone. The North Wales Police are looking to hire Polish-speaking officers with sufficient English language competency to serve in predominantly Polish neighborhoods.

Estimates of the number of Poles living in Scotland range from 40,000 to 100,000. Of that number 8,000 live in Edinburgh, with the rest distributed in towns with factory jobs. These companies have a bonafide need for workers. Scotland's own youth have long been leaving in droves to seek better jobs elsewhere, so in this case immigrants really DO take the jobs the locals don't want to fill.

As an unintended, but not unwelcome, consequence, unlike France, Germany and Italy which have birth rates below population replacement levels, Scotland has just proclaimed that immigrants from Eastern Europe have triggered a baby boom. Births in Scotland in the first three months of 2007 went up by 646 over the first quarter of 2006. Of those 646 babies, 20 percent were born to mothers from Eastern Europe. The majority of that number were born to Polish parents. Yes, parents. Married couples. People who go to church.

The impact, which Polish migrants are having on Catholic, churches in England, Scotland Wales and Ireland is nothing short of astounding. In some neighborhood parishes, masses in Polish are held with standing room only crowds. Even some Cathedrals are beginning to bulge at the seams on Sundays. Indeed, this influx of Catholicism seems to be on a demographic course to overturn Anglicanism as the dominant religion in Britain. Holy Henry the Eighth.

So great is the demand for Polish speaking clergy, that the Roman Catholic Church has sent at least one prominent

Bishop to recruit (poach) priests from Poland. Where there are staffing shortfalls, Polish clergy are sent out to visit parishes on a rotating basis like the circuit riding preachers in America's colonial days once were. Beyond worship services, these congregations offer a support network where members can share insights on living in a country with different social and economic parameters. They ease homesickness while reinforcing traditional values. In other words, Catholicism is providing faith-based assimilation.

Because they are far apart in generational terms, young Polish immigrants have not networked much with the "Oldies," those who arrived in England after the Second World War. Making connections with their peers is being made easier through a growing number of Polish social clubs. The Polish Cultural and Social Institute in the London district of Hammersmith frequently host special events. New media outlets such as the London-based paper Polish newspaper, Cooltura, are also facilitating resources for jobs, cultural events and practical advice. A handful of Internet sites give leads on sharing rentals and dating, as well as posting news headlines from back home. See for example: (www.toplanguagecommunity.com)

Special job fairs cater to the needs of young Polish workers. 5000 of them turned up to attend the third Annual Recruitment fair in London. The host of this event is The Polish Express, known as the newspaper for "the Polish Diaspora."

To be fair, not all the lives of Polish immigrants have been rosy. Many with poor language skills have been shunted into job ghettos, primarily in the building trades. Others have found adjusting to life in Britain simply too hard and have packed it in. The already over taxed British health care system is experiencing a strain from immigrant overload. There are a few xenophobes who speak out on occasion against this "hoard of invading Poles." But the overwhelming impression is that the UK could do worse than having a surge of decent hard working immigrants arriving on their shores. In a newspaper article from that previously mentioned town in Wales, one man commented:

"We are lucky to be the focus of Polish immigration; you hear foreign words in Wrexham, look up and see a nice looking young couple doing their shopping, they seem to be decent hard working people looking for a better life, and you can't help thinking there are a lot worse in our society, even the ones born here. Don't forget that the Poles who come here are the go-getters who don't sit at home moaning, they have made an effort to improve themselves, I wish we had more people with that spirit."

One is moved to observe that this immigration story makes a rather nice counterpoint to the sounds of civilizations clashing!

July 7, 2007

Emperor Sarkozy?

He was President of France for barely a month when the socialist newspaper, Liberation, called for Nicholas Sarkozy to give up jogging because "it is a capitalist pastime designed to undermine serious thought and democracy." This gave rise to a national outburst of blogging on whether running was, in fact, right wing. The French magazine, Marrianne, took aim from another angle. It published side-by-side portraits of Sarkozy and Napoleon III. The inference was obvious. The Emperor of France from 1852-1870, Napoleon III was an authoritarian figure who practiced relentless self-aggrandizement. Some pundits have begun to wonder if Sarkozy, who seems to share those character traits, is angling to become the first Emperor of Europe. He is certainly a man on the run and that grandiose job title is not just a wild-eyed flight of fancy.

An article in the July 4th edition of The Guardian, England's left leaning broadsheet, proclaimed "Emperor Sarko Leaves PM to be just a messenger." The Prime Minister to which the headline refers is Francois Fillon, the former French Labour Minister. He was the man responsible for the French retirement system and the implementation of the boom busting 35-hour work week policy. Just as the British press loved to tag Tony Blair as George Bush's poodle, Fillon (who -- it must be said -- now jogs daily with Sarko) is already being called a "puppet." Low riders call him Sarkozy's "mini-me." The article asserted that Fillon comes out only to deliver speeches dictated by his boss, and then returns to the shadows (although how long could they be?) cast by the hyperactive and short "Super Sarko." Yet another French publication joined the linguistic fray by coining the word "Tsar-kozy" to describe the new President's governing style. Then, striking real fear in the hearts of militant secularists, Socialist leader Francois Hollande went on a tirade before the French Parliament accusing Sarkozy of exhibiting downright godly qualities. He lashed out at Sarkozy as being: "omnipresent, omnipotent, and omniscient, decides everything, talks about everything, intervenes in everything and is everywhere." Now a word in your ear about Hollande. After the Socialist party candidate -- the fetching Segolene Royal - lost the Presidential election to Sarkozy, she dumped Hollande. He was not just her domestic partner (French for common-law wife), she is also the mother of his four children. Socialist family values.

The accusation that he is everywhere came just after Sarkozy participated in his first European Union meeting in June and then took his first non official, non- European trip, to visit Algeria and Tunisia. For those who were absent from class that day, Algeria was once a French colony and there are lots of hard feelings about the split. More than 1.5 million Algerians died fighting against France for their independence. Again Sarkozy wowed an unsuspecting world with a real grandstand play. He came to state that French industries were now poised to invest -- big time -- in Algeria. He spoke of future joint ventures in power production -- traditional gas reserves, biofuels, and "civil nuclear energy."

Next came the topic of immigrant labor. Since all Polish plumbers and carpenters have presumably left for England, and they are running low on Turks in Germany, Europe is facing a shortage of low level jobbers. Sarkozy seems to favor opening the gates to legal immigrants -- from Muslim countries -- to fill the expected gaps in Europe's workforce over the next two decades.

But wait. There's more.

Before the press could catch its breath, Sarkozy announced that it was time for "La Mediterranean Unity" (MU) which is to be an extension of the EU model. Sarzoky forged ahead and unilaterally invited Southern European and North African leaders to a get together for some alliance-shaping in 2008. The Algerian President, Abdelaziz Bouteflika, stood next to Sarko during this press conference, smiling broadly.

When someone did manage to ask Sarkozy if he was inclined to apologize for the colonial misdeeds of France, he said more than just NO. Algerians today, he explained, "are looking at the future. They do not want their leaders to put everything on hold and engage in self-flagellation for the mistakes or mis-steps of the past."

Sarkozy also made an unprecedented appearance at the annual meeting of ministers for the Euro Area (known as the Euro-Group) on July 9th. Since they created the Euro currency, it seems that NO European head of state ever came to a follow-up meeting to hammer out the details. Not one of them. They voted to go Euro and then left the details to financial wizards who probably studied economics at Hogwarts.

Is it magic that it now costs $1.35 to buy a single Euro? So what's up with Sarkozy nosing his way into this meeting? It is rumored that Sarkozy has his own ideas about how the European Central Bank does business. He also believes that certain trade policies have to be finagled (love that word) to benefit those countries, which signed on to the Euro concept. Can you spell "subsidies?" He is also poised to intervene in a stalled joint European venture involving the manufacturing of airplanes. Alors!

A few weeks ago, speculation had it that Tony Blair was going to become the first President of the European Union. He and Sarkozy were seen exiting a Paris eatery, arm in arm as comrades do, which was interpreted as Sarkozy wanting Tony to become top boy at the EU.

This past week, the European Commission Chief, Jose Manuel Barroso, floridly proclaimed: "The EU is not just any old international organization, nor is it a super state, but it might just be an Empire." To which he added for emphasis: "We are a very special construction, unique in the history of mankind."

On Bastille Day, (Saturday July 14th) Sarkozy led the traditional parade down the Champs Elysees. Escorted by mounted regiments of the French Republic Guards, he stood up in the back of a French military vehicle as it passed around the Arc de Triomphe. Behind him -- at his invitation -- marched troops from the 26 other European Union nations. It is the first time such a military display was ever coordinated.

For some time there has been chatter about creating an EU Army. Just days before this major French holiday, Sarkozy gave a speech to a gathering of European defense ministers and military officers. "The basis for a European defense exists. We must make it grow," Sarkozy said, "I want Europe to be capable of ensuring its security autonomously." Emphasis on the "I."

"It was a parade of armies but it is peace that we want to celebrate," he explained.

July 16, 2007

Sense and Solidarity for Poland

How many of you knew that the President of Poland came to America on July 16?

Thought so. This state visit was essentially overlooked by the media. Poland has a long history of being treated like the Rodney Dangerfield of nations. As far back as the 18th century, historians referred to "The Negative Poland Policy," the European practice of bribing noblemen to keep this besieged country no more than an agricultural backwater. When it joined the European Union in 2004, after decades of Soviet domination, the hope was that Poland was finally going to get the respect it deserved.

Indeed, the twin brothers Kaczynski who preside over the current government, President Lech and Prime Minister Jaroslav respectively, have been acting up and speaking out, but Brussels seems determined to hit Poland where it hurts the most and muffle the mouse before roaring becomes a bad habit. At summits for example.

Jaws dropped in June at the European Union (EU) meeting when Poland complained that the voting rules for member nations were unfair because they were based on population size. We would have more citizens and greater voting rights if the Germans hadn't killed so many of us during World War Two, said the Poles. Not since John Cleese goose-stepped around the lobby of Faulty Towers had such an anti-German comment been paraded out in public. One of the EU's foremost club rules is: "Don't Mention the War." Germany's Chancellor Angela Merkel, who held the rotating EU Presidency and was thus hosting this event, must have been livid.

By mid-June, Russian President Vladimir Putin was none too happy with Poland either. The brothers Kaczynski had angered the Russian government by offering America some land on which to construct part of a proposed new missile defense system. The Russians didn't buy the sales pitch that the missiles these facilities would house would not be directed at Russia, but at "rogue" states such as North Korea and Iran. Small surprise then that Russian news sources put a chilly spin on the warm reception President Bush gave his Polish counterpart in Washington last week. Poland was said to be "courting" America, trying to overcome its incredible bad luck. They could be on to something.

After his stop over in Washington, D.C., President Kaczynski toured Vandenberg Air Force Base in Santa Barbara, California, looking over the kinds of equipment that the missile shield will require. His genial comments about US-Polish cooperation belied polls, conducted by a publicly funded institute in Warsaw, which indicate that 55 percent of the Polish people opposed hosting a U.S. missile defense base on their turf. The deal had also been offered without the advice and consent of the Polish parliament. This occasioned a vociferous outcry for a public referendum on the proposed project, but that may not happen if the US cannot submit to a rather significant Polish demand. Speaking to the press about security concerns, the head of Poland's National Security Bureau, Wladyslaw Stasiak, stated that the proposed US base, and all its personnel, would have to agree to abide completely by Polish law versus being what is known as "extraterritorial." There could be no immunity, no exceptions, and no negotiating on the point, thank you. This is a mighty big condition for the mouse to propose to the lion, but a peace offering was in hand. This came when President Kaczynski posthumously awarded Poland's highest honor, The White Eagle, to the late President Ronald Reagan. The audience at the Reagan Presidential Library cheered as Nancy Reagan accepted the award.

But the cheers had barely faded away in Simi Valley, CA, when, back in Europe, Brussels made its own rather stunning demand on the Kaczynski administration. After Poland joined the EU, it continued to heavily subsidize its three main shipyards. This indisputably violated EU regulations limiting state aid, by any EU member nation, to one of its own key industrial sectors. Poland was able to strike a deal for two of its shipyards, Gyynia and Szczecin. In those cases, the EU forgave state subsidies in exchange for cutbacks in capacity. But no deal was ever put forth to resolve the situation at the third -- and most important entity -- the Gdansk shipyard, birthplace of the Solidarity Movement.

It was not unexpected but nonetheless unwelcome when, on July 21, the European Union Competition Commissioner gave Polish authorities 30 days to either close two of the three shipways at Gdansk or repay, to the EU, the accumulated state aid which Gdansk has received. By all accounts this amounts to 192 million zlotys or $71 million US. The initial response of the Polish deputy economics minister in charge of the shipyard sector was to wail about imminent bankruptcy and loss of jobs. Authorities in Poland then floated the idea that there had been an unwritten agreement that Poland would have two extra years to sort out the Gdansk problem -- a proposition quickly denied by EU officials. Some Poles wondered if the price of EU membership was worth sacrificing sacred ground. The question is -- just how sacred is this place? The Gdansk shipyard, which sits on prime Baltic Coast real estate and is surrounded by the city's historic old town area, is the target of developers who want to build condos on or near this hallowed ground.

Roman Galezewski, a member of the board for the Gdansk yard, said that the invocation of the EU's competition rules were a diversion. Far from being concerned with enforcing competitive policies, Galezewski asserted that EU officials were acting on behalf of a US investment fund which has already purchased the yard's land from the Gdansk City Hall. "Ever since the massive value of the land bought by the American fund from the city has become known, everything possible has been done to shut down the yards," Galezewski insisted.

The EU has received assurances from the Kaczynski administration that a response to their ultimatum will arrive by August 21. Will the shipyards give way to bulldozers and building cranes? Can the mouse roar loudly enough to stop the developers or is it willing to sacrifice solidarnosc for profit? Can the movement which helped end Soviet communism rise up again to block the construction of pricey condos? Is Pope John Paul II spinning in his Vatican grave?

July 26, 2007

Why the Floods in Britain Have Not Been Gordon Brown's Katrina

Three years ago, Hurricanes Katrina and Rita scored back-to-back hits on the Gulf coast. During the storms, wild rumors combined with hyped and grossly inaccurate news stories made seasoned reporters seem like Chicken Littles on speed. Despite the fact that hurricane relief efforts in the US are mandated to begin on the local, then county and state, and lastly at the federal level, the Bush Administration was attacked as if it was supposed to be running everything from the get-go. Congress and the press kept up the partisan drumbeats and managed to turn an act of God into a political vendetta.

This has not been the case across the pond where, in late July, record-breaking floods washed over vast swathes of the UK countryside. The Head of International Logistics for the British Red Cross said his people had to mount the largest on-the-ground response on UK soil since World War Two. On a single day, 141 flights in and out of Heathrow airport were canceled. London Underground stations and commuter trains experienced delays and closures. Motorists were stranded. Every existing emergency service was taxed to its limits across the British midlands. In Gloucestershire alone, 140,000 people had no running water for a week. Miraculously, only a few people died, including a set of premature twins when their Mother was trapped by rising water.

Granted, Gordon Brown has been Prime Minister for only a month, but he has served for ten years at the top of Blair's New Labour government. The record shows Labour had many warnings and the time to plan ahead for disaster. So why did Bush get bashed (and labeled as an indifferent racist) over Katrina, while Gordon Brown seems to have walked on the waters which turned English towns into islands? One didn't expect a peep out of the left leaning British media, but where were the voices of the opposition shouting "off with his head." Where was the outcry from the masses?

Curiously, it was Conservatives who began hinting to reporters that their Party leader, David Cameron (who was visiting Rwanda during the rains) ought to consider stepping down for the good of their party. Yes, presented with the opportunity to take the higher (and drier) ground by attacking the Labour Party's disaster planning failures, the Tories fell silent. The result is that Brown's post-flood poll numbers have gone up. The press now cheerfully reports that if Brown decides to call a snap election in the fall, he will win. Cameron, whose constituencies were seriously submerged by the monsoon conditions, mumbled something about how the shine on the new Prime Minister would soon begin to tarnish. Perhaps he should have said "rust." It was vintage Alice through the looking glass politics on the Thames.

No my friends, Gordon Brown neither apologized for the Labour government's failures in disaster planning, nor comforted the nation on TV or radio. Aside from the kinds of generic promises one expects (about which more later), Brown said precious little. Well, he was heard to tell a group of exhausted disaster relief workers, "You've done brilliantly. We're really proud."

But Brown & Co. have a lot of 'splaining to do. Here's the back-story. Throughout the 1990's, the former chief executive of the UK's Environmental Agency, Ed Gallagher, repeatedly warned the government that the UK's flood defenses were insufficient and increasingly vulnerable. New Labour took office in 1997 and the Blair government was told, by any number of its own Ministers, that Victorian era sewers were bound to give way the next time severe flooding occurred. Informed about these inevitable calamities, one of Brown's first actions at the Treasury was to cut the budget for the Environmental Agency. Heavy rains came in 1998 and again in 2000. In their wake, Labourites were unmoved. None seems to have suggested a system for collecting excess water and providing drainage to handle the regular UK cycle of rain and droughts. Hello global warming fans - these cycles go back to when records started being kept in 1766. Instead, Labour went for the boom and ignored history. Real estate developers were allowed to build large houses up to the edges of rivers and on known flood plains. No laws obliged them to design elevated homes (or stilted as they once were known) with living areas a floor above potentially rising waters. No laws were passed which required utility companies to review flood defenses at their major plants and consider moving them to higher ground.

In communities given the option of voting on better flood defenses, the common good fell victim to the "not in my back yard" syndrome. Labour was also successfully lobbied by environmentalists who insisted that flood barriers would inflict "unforgivable damage" on protected stretches of property known as "greenbelt areas."

First off her mark in the July 07 crisis was Lady (Baroness) Young who received her peerage for giving $trong $upport to the Labour Party. In her role as the current head of the UK's Environmental Agency, Lady Young proclaimed that water bills would immediately have to be raised to pay for improving drainage and protecting infrastructure. This came as a low blow to consumers because the water industry has been imposing above-inflation rate increases on UK householders for the past several years. The Severn Trent Water Company, which serves an area seriously impacted by the July floods, reported $600 million (£300 mil) in profits last year. This was not a one-off sum amassed by a single corporate water entity. OFWAT, the agency responsible for oversight of the UK's water industry, reported that water supplying companies were supposed to spend a combined total $8.6 billion (£4.3 bil) in infrastructure improvements from 2005-06, but fell $2 billion short (£1 bil). No one seems to know why.

Swiftly, Lady Young's predecessor, Ed Gallagher, resurfaced on the BBC to ask the Environmental Agency's managers to refund their annual five figure bonuses. Young's bonus amounts to $48,000, 15% of her annual salary of $326,000 (£163,000).

Alistair Darling, Brown's successor as Treasury Secretary, stood up to say that businesses and people affected by the floods would be given extra time to pay taxes and that interest and surcharges on late payments would be waived. Very kind indeed.

Gordon Brown promised that funds would immediately be made available to flood-hit councils and promised all local authorities would receive 100 per cent compensation. That's some high-ticket promise as economists estimate the July floods will total $10 billion (£5 billion) or more in damage claims.

Brown also vowed to crank up the government's budget for flood protection to £800 mil annually by 2010-11. One wonders about that. This is the same period over which the residents of the UK are supposed to help pay for the facilities needed to host the 2012 Olympics. Will Peter be robbed downriver to pay Paul?

The Mayors of Tewkesbury and Gloucester, whose towns were severely affected by flooding, evidenced some real moxey. After the enormous sums the British people have raised for disasters like the 2004 tsunami, these two gents felt it was time to ask for relief money from their own people. And they did. So far the Mayors' Flood Appeal has taken in £250,000 ($500K).

During the deluge, the famous British sense of humor surfaced occasionally. The Times of London columnist, David Aaronovitch, wrote an editorial which lampooned his own newspaper for running the headline: The Floods -- What Went Wrong? His answer was -- "It rained a hell of a lot." To those who suggested that the government ought to have done more, he asked them to imagine Gordon Brown leading the members of Parliament down to the river banks where they would lay like human sandbags to stem the rising tides.

One presumes this is funny because the Brits have become so accustomed to bad government that expectations, unlike rainfall totals, are at an all time low. Scan the newspaper commentaries and only a handful wonder where support from the European Union might be. Was disaster relief something Tony Blair waived as an EU membership benefit for Britain?

"Our governments tend to stumble on from one calamity to the next. That is why the Empire is no more," lamented a blogging Brit whose stiff upper lip now fails him.

August 3, 2007

Mother Knows All the Best Games

In French one speaks of "les vacances." This plural for "vacation" reflects cultural reality. The French take several holidays every year. Paris is a virtual ghost town for the entire month of August, so it was a sure bet that the new President of France and his family would get out of town too. Since one of the Presidential perks is access to an official residence on the Mediterranean, the French assumed the Sarkozys would avail themselves of that venue. It would be a step up from Arcachon, a city in south-west France famed for its oyster farms, where the Sarkozys have spent the previous three summers.

Instead the Sarkozys eschewed the oysters, nixed the Med, and opted for an American holiday. The family accepted an invitation to stay in a luxury villa on Lake Winnipesaukee, in Wolfeboro, New Hampshire. It is one of this nation's oldest vacation spots and also happens to be an hour's drive from the Bush family digs in Kennebunkport, Maine. The decision triggered a French national identity crisis.

"Sarkozy's Holiday in US Raises Eyebrows," read one French newspaper headline. Eyebrows my Aunt Fanny. As soon as the news hit the Rue, the French media began howling with righteous Gallic indignation. The newspaper, Le Monde, sniffed that Sarkozy had clearly embarked on a unilateral mission to improve Franco-American relations, strained since the Chirac government objected to the US invasion of Iraq. Shocking! Another paper wagged its editorial finger and said that a holiday in America proved Sarkozy's critics were right to label him as an "Atlanticist." Another commentator warned that by going to New Hampshire, Sarkozy "risked horrifying the historically anti-American French establishment." The worst came from a commentator who predicted that -- ALORS -- Sarkozy wanted to become the French Margaret Thatcher.

The Socialists also fumed over this vacation. They decried Sarkozy's attraction to American style displays of conspicuous consumption. The Left has taken every opportunity to publish a list of Sarkozy's billionaire friends -- their names and what they own. Naturally, they demanded to know who was paying for this trip. A spokesperson for Sarkozy dutifully reported that the family had taken a commercial flight to the US and that the owner of the villa, an American and a former Microsoft official, had offered them use of the place, which rents for $30,000 a week, as a gift. This generated more outrage. Who gives gifts like this to the President of France? What will they want in return? (A blueprint for an exceptionally safe and efficient French nuclear power plant might be nice.) One political observer lamented that, in the 100 days since he took office, Sarkozy had turned the elegant French Presidency into a sordid reality TV show.

Sarkozy has often commented that his family history has made him feel like an outsider in his own country. His Father was a minor aristocratic Hungarian refugee who escaped the Soviets by joining the French Foreign Legion. His French Mother's heritage goes back to the medieval expulsion of the Jews from the south of France. Nicholas was five when his parents divorced. He grew up in the Paris home of his Jewish grandfather, a respected physician. Although he has a degree in law, Nicholas Sarkozy never attended the schools of the elite. In these institutions, French insiders routinely turn over the reigns of various powerful bureaucracies to the next generation. Small wonder that America's ethos and freedoms from class restrictions would hold a fascination for this man.

His family history explains why Sarkozy interrupted his American idyll and flew back to France to lead mourners at the funeral of the 80-year-old retired Archbishop of Paris, Cardinal Jean Marie Lustier. Like Sarkozy's grandfather, Lustiger was a Jew who converted to Catholicism.

For the President of France to attend this particular funeral was a cultural marker. France is an avowed secular society and it does have its issues with Muslims, but government control over religious matters is standard practice. The French government deported Muslim Imams who were determined to be preaching hatred and terrorism in their mosques. Guidelines to measure the radicalism of an Imam were government created and enforced. The French government has approved religious studies curriculums in public schools. Muslim girls are not allowed to wear headscarves to classes. On the other hand, Christians are not allowed to wear crucifixes, not Jews their yarmulkes in any government-sponsored institution. France has a different way of really separating church and state.

On this side of the Atlantic, Wolfeboro's town website posted a banner to "Welcome Nicolas Sarkozy!!" Winnepesaukee means "smile of the great spirit," but there was no smile on the face of the French President just days after his arrival. A couple of photographers had gotten a little too close for Sarkozy's comfort and a picture of him extending his arm in anger made the Drudge Report. On his radio show, Matt quipped -- "Like they don't have paparazzi in Paris? Ask Princess Di."

After Sarkozy returned from his overnight trip to lead Cardinal Lustiger's funeral, he made the quick trip to Kennebunkport. During their informal chat, President Bush, who has never vacationed outside the United States, made another of his infamous gaffes. He told Sarkozy he would consider taking a holiday in France if he could ride his mountain bike there. Would someone please tell the leader of the Free World about the French Alps? Mrs. Sarkozy spared herself this display of geographical ignorance and proffered menu of hot dogs. She called Laura Bush to beg off because she had a sore throat, but was seen that same day, in Wolfeboro, shopping with her children. The proprietor of the local cheese shop had told reporters he hoped she would drop in. You cannot make this up.

When they returned to Paris, the blogs heated up again. Sarkozy promised the French that if they loved Jackie Kennedy Onassis, they would love Cecillia. But her presumed snub of the Bushes was not well received in the French Press. It is not that the French like Bush, but this exhibition of bad manners was judged an embarrassment to the nation. Go figure.

Now that he is back in France, Sarkozy is facing some interesting challenges. He gave in to pressure and will allow an inquiry on his dealings with the government of Libya. He denies that there was any connection between the release of Bulgarian nurses -- being held on charges that they spread AIDS with contaminated needles -- and the sale to Libya of anti tank missiles and nuclear technology which is supposed to be used to desalinate water. Mrs. Sarkozy led the vanguard on this exchange. The Unions have promised to block Sarkozy's announced reforms which might cut into the French multiple vacation culture and the endless array of government subsidies and benefits.

Still, a recent poll indicated that 64% of the French public approves of Sarkozy's hyper- Presidential pace and his flair for the dramatic. His fellow citizens seem more concerned about whether or not he can keep up the pace he has set for himself so far.

August 17, 2007

Chillary

"Hillary is the first choice of Martian visitors," or so said Gerard Baker in his August 17 Op Ed piece in The Times of London. Baker, who is the U.S. Editor of the Times, reports that wherever he went across Europe this summer everyone asked him the same question: "who's going to win the election?" Baker attributes this to a unique confluence of interest between Europe and the States. "However briefly," he writes, "the rest of the world is thinking the same way as America."

Baker admits that this is not a question he would normally feel comfortable answering, especially since the election is fully 15 months away. Who among us enduring this era of the eternal campaign cannot empathize? But what do Martians have to do with anything?

The humorous galactic gambit is Baker's way of stating the bloody obvious. If a Martian were to come down and follow the Democrat Party's US Presidential candidates for a few days, he would wonder why there was any question at all why Mrs. Clinton should not be the anointed. "It is evident that she is the most knowledgeable, experienced and disciplined. Most of the time, like a Queen Elizabeth I or a Margaret Thatcher, she easily dominates the inferior men shuffling around her," states Baker. He then hastens to add that she is not his favorite person. "I continue to find the ease with which she has sacrificed her principles on everything of importance, the makeover from radical feminist to soft-focused mother and devoted wife, from V-sign-waving peacenik to hawkish warmonger, all a little chilling even for my slightly cynical tastes." Baker laments the credulity of American voters who are likely to overlook Hillary's faults.

"To be fair for a moment," Baker concludes, "even I would have to acknowledge that Bill Clinton's First Lady (though, assuredly not his last), on the evidence of the campaign so far at least, deserves her lead."

He sees the lesser Democrat candidates as merely hanging around in a tedious collective audition for spots in Mrs. Clinton's Administration.

Baker is dismissive of Barack Obama. "To be frank," he says, "that same Martian would have to wonder what exactly all the fuss was about with the Illinois Senator." He rejects the endless comparisons between Obama and JFK adding: "Mr. Obama remains an oddly unconvincing world saviour." Nor does Baker spare candidate John Edwards. He characterizes the Edwards campaign as "larded with a hypocrisy and opportunism that make Mrs. Clinton look like St. Thomas More."

In June, another London Times reporter, Sarah Baxter, penned a book review of political consultant, Bob Schrum's, mid life memoir: "No Excuses: Confessions of a Serial Campaigner." With the eye catching headline: "Clinton's zipper problem returns to haunt Hillary," Baxter chose to indicate the gossipy nature of Schrum's tome by recounting the late Pamela Harriman's fury at Bill Clinton. The story goes that he once brought a woman back to Harriman's home to spend the night with him. Harriman, then the US Ambassador to France, had quite a reputation as what is called a "courtesan" in polite company, but even she was repulsed by Bill Clinton's recklessness. Baxter's slant on Hillary's candidacy is that it will put the spotlight back on the Clinton's clearly rocky marital history, something rhetorically echoed in the words of Michele Obama last weekend: "If you can't run your own house, you can't run the White House."

In his August 19 commentary on Hillary, The Independent's Foreign Editor, Leonard Doyle, asks: "Why Is She Hated By Progressives and Right Wingers Alike?" His subtitle gives the answer straightaway. "They say she is a scheming control-freak who will stop at nothing in her bid to become the first Mrs. President." For the record, The Independent is the youngest (founded 1986) of the UK's daily papers. It was begun by former Telegraph journalists as an alternative venue for those who did not subscribe to the world-view of the Murdoch publishing cartel. It is positioned to attract readers who are politically center left, which suggests it should be aligned with Mrs. Clinton. But Doyle chose to pack his Hillary piece with rather unflattering snippets. Not least of these is his focus on how Hillary has riled America's left wing feminists. Doyle cites best selling author and filmmaker Nora Ephron as an exemplar of this crowd. Once a supporter who said someone would have to burn down the White House to get her to say anything against the former First Lady, now Ephron is an avowed Hillary resister. Why? Because, she says, (in so many words) you can't trust Hillary as far as you can spit. This turn hinges almost entirely on the New York Senator's position on the war in Iraq, frequently cited as the probable source of her downfall, should it come. And here's a slam which Doyle saw fit to print, although it is unlikely to appear in the New York Times. He quotes Jane Fonda's description of Hillary as "a ventriloquist for the patriarchy with a skirt and a vagina." One could argue with the skirt comment as Hillary is always seen wearing pantsuits.

The Guardian newspaper, demographically positioned for center to left wing readers, warned its audience that whoever was elected President in 08, one regrettable fact would not change. A June 7 article remorsefully noted that, even when the evangelical Bush left office, there would be no escape from Christianity. That piece (with an embedded sigh) was entitled: "There's one thing the US presidential contenders all have in common: God." Two weeks later, a Guardian correspondent posted in Washington held out hope for British lefties by reporting: "Poll of Democrats reveals Gore could still steal the show." This political resurrection, should it happen, was put down to "the greatest brand makeover in history."

For pure comic relief, the Times ran a contribution from the witty Hugo Rifkind, who specializes in writing humorous send-ups of celebrities. In this instance, Rifkind conjured up an uncomplimentary image of Hillary (and Bill) by creating a week's worth of imaginary entries from her personal diary.

Here are two excerpts from Monday -- with the really juicy bits edited out.

"I am dressing. My husband, Bill, is still in bed, watching a women's beach volleyball match on TV."

"I am not one of those apple-pie women who frets over her white slacks and gingham shirt each day. Hell no. I despise those women. Although I also respect them, as Americans. Today, though, I'm not sure. Should I be Soft Hillary, in pink and beige, with a glimpse of flesh? Or should I be Hard Hillary?"

It is this impression of Mrs. Clinton which led a Telegraph writer to nickname her "the power behind the drone."

But for all the insults and parodies being aimed at Hillary and Obama et. al, the respected European journal, The Economist, reports that 40% of GOP supporters believe the Democrats will win the White House in 2008. That is no laughing matter.

August 27, 2007

Jihad, Comedy and Life

Did you read about the outrageous stunt staged last week in Australia (not Austria), site of the APEC (not OPEC) conference? For the sake of security, $130 million was spent on erecting a "ring of steel" around the summit venue. Nonetheless, a three-car motorcade, which featured an Osama bin Laden look-alike, made it through two police checkpoints and stopped very near to the hotel where President Bush was staying.

The merry Aussie pranksters were from the Australian Broadcasting Company's satirical TV program, The Chasers. While the crew were being arrested, (and Osama's fake beard was being confiscated) the police told them how lucky they all were not to have been taken out by sniper fire. The show's producer, Julian Morrow, replied that the security people were lucky these were not real Al Qaeda guys. The police were heard chuckling while they chastised the group. The incident might easily have become another urban legend, but the cameraman held on to his tape and there was film at 11.

An editorial in the (Australian) newspaper, The Orstrahyun, observed that while the summit authorities were livid over being mocked, most of the rest of Sydney was cheered by this moment of sheer comic relief. The Chasers bold gate crashing had provided, "a good laugh to the miserable, repressive atmosphere forced on us by the blocked roads, blocked footpaths, snipers leaning out of hovering helicopters and the endless violations of privacy thousands of workers in the city are being subjected to on a daily basis, with demands to see ID, physical searches in city streets and briefcases and handbags opened and emptied." This entire episode recalls the slogan which the Pogo comic strip made famous: "We have met the enemy and he is us."

An American comedian, Lewis Black, recently made an astute observation in an online comedy blog. "The difference between our country and Afghanistan is that Afghanistan didn't have any comedians. They were very serious about everything and things went awry. Their whole country was doomed because they didn't have any comedians to point out what was unbalanced about their culture."

There are encouraging signs that - in Western societies - Muslim humor exists and may even be a growth industry. There is, for example, a touring Muslim comedy troop who call themselves "Allah Made Me Funny." The Canadian Broadcasting Company premiered a new "light hearted" sitcom. In "Little Mosque on the Prairie" the Muslim and non Muslim citizens of a town named Mercy overcome misunderstandings as they interact. The show's creators expressed a hope that their sitcom could someday become the Islamic version of Seinfeld. Australian author Randa Abdel-Fattah has written a coming of age story about a young Muslim. girl who struggles with wearing her headscarf (hijab) – full time - to the new public school she must attend. The book's title is "Does My Head Look Big in This?" It is warm and funny and insightful.

Things tend to be a little more tense in Europe. Oddly enough, September 12th is the first anniversary of Pope Benedict's lecture at his old university in Germany. There he quoted from an historic source document which criticized an aspect of Islam. This single sentence evoked protests galore and resulted in the murder of a nun. And let's not forget the worldwide kefuffle in 2005 over a dozen Danish editorial cartoons, the majority of which featured less than flattering images of Muhammad.

Given this Islamic proclivity for over-reaction, audiences at the Edinburgh Fringe Festival, held in Scotland this August, might well have expected to be literally blown away by Jihad: The Musical. The show was a wild and scathing parody of all things held holy, one might say, by Islamic radicals. Jihad: The Musical featured a chorus line of women clad is neon pink burkas whirling those curved Middle Eastern swords around as they danced. The central character is an Afghani flower seller, Sayid Al Boom, who gets sucked into a terrorist cell and is encouraged to become a suicide bomber. He is followed by a Fox reporter who also encourages him in this new path as long as she gets the exclusive rights to film his indoctrination in order to become a media star herself. Reviews were mixed, but one had to admire the guts it took to stage the production.

Downloads of the production - including such delightful tunes as "The Jihad Jive," "The Suicide Song," and "I Wanna Be Like Osama" can be found on YouTube.com or at www.jihad-the-musical.com.

Jihad was, in its fashion, a tribute to Mel Brooks' 1968 film, The Producers. It had been scant 20 years since the end of World War II and the Holocaust, but Brooks' took an inspired risk to illustrate that laughing at one's enemies can be empowering. The sight of a goose-stepping chorus line, marching in swastika formation to the lilting tune of "Springtime for Hitler," undoubtedly shocked some people, but getting the proverbial last laugh did prove liberating. The Producers has since become a cottage industry of sorts. Still, the comedy divide in this clash of civilizations remains skewed in our direction. When God turned up in a movie in the form of a cigar puffing George Burns, not even the most over-the-top evangelical Christian threatened to behead anyone. By comparison, in the past week, a group of Muslim fanatics announced it would be their pleasure to lop off the heads of Madonna and Britney Spears to stop them from strutting their satanic stuff. In retaliation, one can still order up Taliban Barbie Dolls in time for Christmas delivery. No lead paint on those burka babes.

Yes, the world was changed forever on September 11, 2001, but worlds are always being changed. Wars, genocides, assassinations, and natural disasters seem unlikely caverns from which gag writers can mine for laughs, but they are. With distance, it is humanly possible to extract some humor from what the unspeakable and unfathomable leave in their wake. When an enemy is pious and pompous, they become especially easy targets for good punch lines. Like the one about how there are no recidivist suicide bombers....That was a well placed zinger from a really great stand-up guy - Donald Rumsfeld.

September 17, 2007

The 9-11 Incident in Brussels

The sixth commemoration of the terrorist attacks on America did not go quietly in Brussels, Belgium, home of the European Parliament. Earlier this year, Stop The Islamisation of Europe (SIOE) applied to the city government of Brussels for a permit to hold a 9-11 memorial demonstration. The Mayor of Brussels, Freddy Thielemans, reviews all such requests. He receives between 500 and 600 every year. In the past six years, he has only turned down six. SIOE 's rejection brought that number up to seven and set off a series of events which led to the 9-11 incident in Brussels.

First some background. The SIOE movement began in Denmark (SIAD - Stop Islamificering Af Danmark). There are now branches in England, France, and Belgium, with others expected to open soon in the Czech Republic, Poland, and Russia. SIOE's website declares that it was formed to prevent Islam from becoming a dominant political force in Europe. SIOE's slogan is: "Racism is the lowest form of stupidity. Islamophobia is the height of common sense." It also has a battle cry: "Enough is Enough. No Sharia Here! Democracy not Theocracy!"

SIOE's position is that all religions should be treated equally by the law, but because Islam is a combined political, legal, and judicial system -- administered and overseen by un-elected theologians -- it is completely contrary to Western concepts of democracy. Islam seeks to be treated differently or in a superior manner. Therefore, Islam and democracy are incompatible.

That's as may be, but the Muslim community in Brussels seems to have no trouble at all participating in the electoral process. The Belgian political party to which Mayor Freddy Thielemans belongs is the Parti Socialiste (PS). It is the largest party in Brussels. It holds 17 of the 47 seats in the city council. 10 of those 17 PS councilors are Muslims. The PS governs Brussels in a coalition with the Christian Democrats who have 11 councilors, of whom 2 are Muslims and 3 are immigrants from sub Saharan Africa. Only 13 of the 27 councilors within the governing coalition are native Belgians. Over half of the inhabitants of the Brussels region are of foreign origin, many of them from Morocco.

In denying SIOE's application to stage a 9-11 memorial gathering, Mayor Thielemans said that he felt the "ethnic" community in Brussels would not tolerate a demonstration which denounced the process by which Europe would morph into Eurabia. He said he was afraid SIOE's presence would spark rioting. In response, SOIE posted an Open Letter of Protest to the Mayor on its website on 15 August. It also created an online petition for others to voice their support. 10,000 signatures were gathered.

Anyone familiar with Mayor Freddy Thielemans would have expected SIOE's petition to fall on deaf ears. Mayor Freddy makes no secret of the fact that he is an atheist with a soft spot for Muslims and a hatred of Christians. On the day that Pope John Paul II died, the news came to Freddy at a cocktail party which included the Mayor of Angouleme, France. He ordered "Champagne for Everyone." A French colleague at the party walked out in disgust. Seems the fellow was Catholic.

Local wags quipped that Freddy (who coincidently celebrated his 63rd birthday on 9-11) was afraid Pope Benedict would die on that very day and he'd have to offer to buy champagne again for everyone. That would be easy if the town square was filled with non-drinking Muslims, but since SIOE was predicting the arrival of 20,000 protestors, old Freddy could have gone bankrupt filling their glasses.

SIOE appealed the denial for their demonstration to several courts, all of which upheld the ban. The leaders of the SIOE then decided their only choice was to march, as an act of civil disobedience, to illustrate how the EU can selectively choose to curb the freedom of expression. News about the event was posted on blogs all over Europe. Worried about that 20,000 figure, Belgian authorities and Mayor Freddy's office again asked SIOE to cancel their plans. They confided that suicide bombers intended to infiltrate their ranks and cause terrible carnage. SIOE was not deterred. Still, when 9-11-07 finally arrived only a few hundred people had assembled for the demonstration.

SIOE's website had listed specific instructions for all participants. They were to assemble in Luxembourg Place. National flags could be carried to indicate European unity for the organization's goals, but no special interest flags or signs, to advance other causes, could be displayed. This point became the spanner in the works.

Vlaams Belang, a group which seeks Flemish independence from Belgium, had offered to join the protest. In return, SIOE promised to support Vlaams Belang in the future. Alas, Vlaams Belang did not keep its word. They brought lots of flags and signs in support of their own independence movement. More egregiously, determined to seize the media spotlight, the Belangers had secretly decided to stage a separate protest for their cause in nearby Schumann Square.

That's when the trouble began. About 100 local policemen had been dispatched to keep things under control, amply armed with riot gear and a water cannon. There is film on YouTube which shows the clash between the police and the Vlaams Belangers. What triggered the clash is not clear, but the footage shows that aggressive police tactics were used in removing the VB protestors from the Square. When the clip was broadcast on TV, file photos of the two main SIOE organizers were meshed with moving images of the Vlaams Belangers being carted away in police buses. SIOE was not amused.

When the dust settled, it was, in fact, the two leaders of the VB Flemish independence group who had been arrested. One is an MEP (Member of the EU Parliament) and the other a VP in the Flemish Parliament. About 120 others were arrested and held for seven hours. Included in that number were also a French MEP and an Italian MEP. Arresting MEP's is a violation of the protocols regarding diplomatic immunity. Italy has already filed a formal complaint. The Italian MEP, Mario Borghezio, told the press: "It doesn't seem normal to me that on the 11th of September, in a European capital, a demonstration… against fundamentalist Islamic terrorism can be banned." For the record, a small number of SIOE demonstrators were eventually allowed to observe a minute of silence outside the EU Parliament building.

The end of the day's events beggars belief. Those who had not been arrested gathered in a cluster of outdoor cafes to discuss what had happened. At some point Mayor Freddy turned up with a small entourage and sat among the SIOE people. A conversation was opened. Although one or two folks suggested he might be a bit of a fascist, Freddy tossed that off and cheerfully offered to pose with anyone who wanted a souvenir photograph taken with him. "We all started to laugh at the absurdity," one SIOE member commented.

SIOE has now disassociated itself from Vlaams Belang and its political agenda. In its official statement, SIOE took no prisoners: "The only way Islamism will be defeated is by fighting it single-mindedly, but you have to have a brain to have a mind, and it's pretty obvious some leaders of some political parties are brainless."

There was scant coverage of this incident in the mainstream European print media, but the websites and blogs of SIOE, its affiliates, and supporters, are now in hyper drive. The debate centers on whether SIOE's denial to peacefully assemble proves their main point. The Mayor of Brussels did not want his Muslim constituency to be offended, ergo the Islamification of Europe is well underway.

SIOE's next big event will be held on October 12. On that day, Muslims who wish to leave the faith (an act punishable by death) are being encouraged to find safety in numbers and become apostates. When asked if SIOE was a right-wing organization, its press spokesperson, Anders Gravers, replied: "Tell me, is it right-wing or left-wing to be against stoning?"

September 18, 2007

Censorship or Fear?

It was on Monday, January 15, 2007, when a line drawn across the Saudi sands also seems to have left a deep and nasty gash on the body of British independence and integrity. At 9 PM that evening, Channel Four, the UK commercial national TV network owned by the BBC, aired a documentary called "Undercover Mosque." The fallout from that 60 minutes of television has become a twisted tale of confused and divided loyalties, a parable of what occurs when multiculturalism goes mad and religion pumps up on steroids. Forget reality TV. This is the real thing.

"Undercover Mosque" was culled from 56 hours of tapes secretly made at various Islamic houses of worship in England. It took nine months to edit the footage. Channel Four believes that some of the comments they recorded can be characterized as incendiary and treasonous. Vociferous critics have labeled it unfair and badly spliced.

The West Midlands Police launched investigations in both directions. The outcome of these inquiries could indicate which way English history is headed. Either the people of the United (or slightly disunited) Kingdom will arise to affirm documents like the Magna Carta (a real copy of which is now on sale for about $20 million) or they will have their national sanctity sold out by the kind of military industrial complex which Ike warned us about way back when.

The asking price for this deal (and a nation's soul) may have been set when military contracts - totaling in the billions of dollars -- were signed by BAE. BAE, a British firm, is Europe's biggest supplier of defense and aerospace equipment. BAE is building the new and improved Royal Saudi Air Force. Hints were dropped to the press that Saudi Prince Bandar (the former ambassador to the United States and close friend of the Bush family) had been paid a substantial "commission" to assure that this lucrative contract was awarded to a UK company. This raised the hairs on the white wigs hanging from the heads of the SFO (the Serious Fraud Office) in Britain. These are the lads and ladettes assigned to keep the government and industry on the straight and narrow. The investigation on what went down between BAE and the Saudi Prince was begun with gusto when suddenly -- PRESTO -- outgoing Prime Minister Tony Blair called off the dogs. Number Ten said to the SFO – "drop it" and it was made so. Zero tolerance in reverse. Next thing you know, Tony Blair is a special envoy to the Middle East. Another story.

But back in January, Channel Four's documentary implied that some of that "finder's fee" to the Prince was being channeled into extremist mosques and stoking the bank accounts of Wahahbist fire breathing imans in England. Some saw the dots connected. Right out of the gate, the documentary makers were charged with racial bias on the basis that they edited the words of three British imams "out of context."

A few quoted phrases prove that cannot be true. In what context does one say things like: "An army of Muslims will arise"... "we must dismantle British democracy".... "we must live like a state within a state until we are strong enough to take over"

Enter the Bobbies. The West Midlands Police, whose territory includes one of the mosques featured in the documentary, then did the wildly unexpected. They reported Channel Four to the media regulator Ofcom (the British version of the FCC) asking them to investigate how the program was edited. The Crown Prosecution Service entered the fray and initially claimed the show "completely distorted" what the imams said.

Kevin Sutcliffe, the commissioning Editor of the Dispatches documentary series, said the West Midland police had produced no evidence to support their claims. "We find it extraordinary that they have gone public on these concerns without discussing them with us first. We believe the comments made in the film speak for themselves -- several speakers were clearly shown making abhorrent and extreme comments."

For the record, Channel Four offered all the speakers whose images and voices were depicted in the film a right to reply and deny that they made these comments. No takers and, says Channel Four, "nor have any of them complained to Ofcom to our knowledge."

Channel Four has further stated that it was fully aware of the sensitivities surrounding the subject matter, particularly its effect on community relations, but believed there was a greater public interest in exposing what was being preached in the name of Islam in some mainstream British mosques.

In blogs linked to articles on Undercover Mosque, there was no shortage of heated discussion. The lurking question was whether or how the West Midlands police came under pressure from Muslims to act against Channel Four, as opposed to investigating the radical imams preaching violence in the mosques. One gentleman asked: "If those imams in the documentary had been Neo-Nazis preaching hatred and war against Muslims, would the police still be taking that stance?" Another gent wrote: "If you don't stand up to bullies, welcome to the concentration camp."

In an official press release, Channel Four observed that Prime Minister Tony Blair had described tolerance as 'what makes Britain Britain' but the Dispatches program clearly reveals how a message of hatred and segregation is being spread throughout the UK and examines how Britain is being influenced by the religious establishment of Saudi Arabia.

Dispatches claims: "The investigation reveals that Saudi Arabian universities are recruiting young Western Muslims to train them in their extreme theology, then sending them back to the West to spread the word". Channel Four further asserts that radical Saudi-trained preachers are promoted in DVD's and books on sale at religious centers in London and other UK cities and that the influence of Wahabism extends beyond the walls of some mosques into influential organizations that advise the British government on inter-community relations and the prevention of terrorism.

The legal waters have been further muddied by the passage of the Racial and Religious Hatred Act of 2006. This legislation makes it a crime to express what is deemed to be "hatred against a person on religious grounds."

Dr. Al Alawi of the Islamic Heritage Foundation has warned: "If this continues, you will have extremist mosques in every corner of the UK. You will not have moderate Muslims walking on our streets anymore."

Winston Churchill is credited with calling the Soviet grip on Eastern Europe "the Iron Curtain." One wonders how he would describe the curtain of political correctness and abject fear which is now enveloping his homeland.

Postscript: Will US justice trump Tony Blair? One of America's most aggressive law firms (Coughlin, Stoia, Geller, Rudman & Robbins) has launched an investigation of the BAE Saudi deal. The charge is that BAE has committed a "systematic abuse of national and international corruption laws." The plaintiffs in the case are the City of Harper Woods Employees Retirement System, a public pension group which holds only a small number of BAE shares. The argument is that BAE's actions constituted a "reckless and negligent breach of their fiduciary responsibilities," causing a devaluation of their share prices, as well as the company's reputation.

October 2, 2007

The Election that Didn't Snap -- How Gordon Lost His Bottle

The British love a good farce, a stage or screen comedy of manners which relies for laughs on improbable situations, innuendoes, misunderstandings, and people flying in and out of doors. Last week the best farce in London-town was performed, not in any West End theatre, but in the halls of Westminster and behind the scenes at Number Ten Downing Street. Everyone had a front row seat to watch as Prime Minister Gordon Brown made a shambles of his authority and reputation. He "lost his bottle" by deciding, at the last minute, not to call a "snap election" in November. That sentence requires a bit of translation.

In the British political system, the office of Prime Minister has no fixed term. A PM is required to call elections every five years, but does not need to step down at that point. He or she can hang on for as long as possible, or until his or her Party turns them out. This generally happens when there is a shift in the political wind or the public outcry for change reaches a dangerously high decibel level.

In the case of Gordon Brown, the office of Prime Minister had been handed to him in June by Tony Blair, who stepped down voluntarily. Brown did not have to call an election for four more years. Despite the fact that Blair's approval rating had hit a low of 23% in 2006, the Labour Party's majority in the House of Commons was secure. Brown had received the mantle of Labour leader by a majority vote of Party members, but the electorate faced years of not having their say on Brown's suitability to hold the post of Prime Minister. This fact was constantly thrown into Brown's craggy face and left the un-elected Prime Minister with the feeling that he needed his own mandate to govern, sooner rather than later. Brown was still enjoying a 100-day honeymoon with the public and press, when he is alleged to have started studying polling data. The figures gave him a good edge over the man who would be his competition for PM, the Tory (Conservative Party) leader, David Cameron. Again, no reason to "snap," but more than anything, Brown wanted to be rid of Tony Blair's shadow.

And so it was that the rumors began to circulate. Brown was going to call a "snap" (capriciously timed and not required) election in early November. Unlike America's now tedious process, a British campaign for choosing a national leader is blessedly brief. It runs for about six weeks. He denied it later, but Brown had clearly set the wheels in motion to mount a "snap election" early on in his tenure. He canceled leaves for his top staffers and began drafting his election manifesto (another British political tradition – a DIY [??]platform written by the candidate and his most trusted inner circle). Instead of "battle buses," the old motor model of creating roving campaign offices on wheels, Brown had reserved a fleet of helicopters and landing spaces for them in London. He was determined to get his people out across the land with lightening speed. It was to be his version of shock and awe. Knowing that the Tories were about to hold their annual Party Conference, (September 30th to October 3rd) Brown flew, unannounced, to Iraq, in order to upstage his opponents. Once on the ground, he made some surprising promises about troop reductions, a move he thought would win him more public favor.

What Brown did not count on was the Miracle at Blackpool, host city of the Tory gathering. Cameron, often characterized as a waffler and a putz, did the unexpected. Taking the stage, Cameron grabbed the mike from its stand, literally leapt from behind the podium, and spent the better part of 90 minutes making a free form speech (no notes, no autocue) to the audience present and to those in the nation watching on their tellies at home. He was positively evangelical. When he finished, Cameron's very attractive wife came up to the stage and embraced him. She whispered into his ear (and conveniently into the open mike he was still wearing) "I love you, Babe." He replied: "I'm knackered," a phrase in British English generally employed to describe one's condition after a long and satisfying bout of lovemaking. This "private exchange" precipitated a seismic shift. Call them fickle, but overnight the British electorate was polled and they were suddenly swooning over Dave.

Gordon Brown, son of a stern Calvinist clergyman, is famous for his gruff manner and insecurities. More than one commentator has referred to him as "the Scottish Hamlet," much prone to brooding. After one such post-Blackpool dark night of the soul, Brown abruptly announced that there would be no snap election. Immediately, the pundits proclaimed that Brown had "lost his bottle." This idiom is Brit speak for a failure of nerve to attempt something at which one was most likely to succeed. By Sunday October 7th, people dressed as brown bottles, with Brown's visage masking their faces, appeared on the streets to ridicule the Prime Minister. Ouch.

Then came Wednesday's regular noon time session in the Commons known as Prime Minster's Question Time during which no-holds-barred volleys are lobbed between the parties. This memorable PMQ began with a Tory from Bromley offering Brown a chance to come to his constituency to see how their recycling efforts handled empty bottles. The Tories could smell blood in the water and Cameron went in for the political kill. Seizing the momentum, Cameron rose across the table from Brown and peppered him with slash and burn remarks. He made much of Brown's latest book, entitled "Courage," and dared him to him gather his own, go to Buckingham Palace, and tell the Queen the snap election was back on.

Throughout Cameron's verbal assault, in typical British fashion, the Tory side of the hall resounded with derisive noises and catcalls. Brown was caught on camera making grimaces and chewing on either gum or his inner cheek linings. At one point, it seemed as if he was going to explode. When he finally rose to his feet, he shouted that he would take no lectures from Cameron who had frequently changed his positions on policies without warning. But Cameron's cool held the day and he sat down looking very much like the proverbial cat that had devoured the canary.

To make matters worse, Alistair Darling, the man who assumed Brown's former job as Chancellor of the Exchequer, made a public speech on the economy in which he simply parroted Tory ideas about tax changes, making it seem as if they were original to the vision of Gordon Brown. No one was fooled for a minute. Political cartoonists depicted Brown and Darling as burglars breaking into a Tory office and rifling the files for their policy papers.

Commentators leaked stories asserting that Tony Blair thought Brown had "made a hash" of things, comparing his performance to the way in which Al Gore had mucked up his Presidential bid in 2000. One wrote: "Tony believes Gordon has gone much too far in trying to distance himself from New Labour's ten years in office. It is where Al Gore went wrong and he is playing into the Tories' hands." Betting parlours began making odds on whether Brown's tenure as PM would be the shortest in British history. Alas for poor Yorick Brown, there is no Oscar, nor a Nobel Peace Prize in his foreseeable future.

A senior Labour Party leader was quoted in the Telegraph as saying: "This has been a major cock-up (more Brit speak) and almost all of our own making." Subsequent polling of marginal constituencies have indicated that Labour's majority would have held firm, but the damage had been done. In the end, it was Gordon Brown, not the election, who seems to have snapped.

But remember, this is a farce, so it should come as no surprise that David Cameron ended his week in California, visiting with Arnold Schwarzenegger. " Look at me and think of Arnold," a puffed up Cameron proclaimed. One clever British reporter took him at his word and created a comparison chart of the two men in his article, pointing out some of the most obvious physical and cultural differences between the Governator and the Tory-Nator. Laughter, stage right.

October 16, 2007

The New Battle of Britain

Fifty years ago, in the quaint second half of the 20th century, some folks in Europe began to imagine that life might be better if their best and brightest were not savagely sacrificed in wars. In place of old-fashioned armed conflicts and brutality, the idea began to emerge that an alliance of nations could be formed to create lasting peace and enhance living conditions through trade and development. The inherent shine began to tarnish as soon as politicians became involved in the implementation process.

The proof is in the numbers. There are 4400 words in the U.S. Constitution. It took 100 days to frame the document. The book edition of the proposed 2004 EU Constitution was 400 pages long although - to be fair - one can obtain a user-friendly PDF file version on the net which only runs 219 pages.

When it was time for the people to have their say, the citizen members of the European Union voted. Several countries said "yes" to the hefty document and the bureaucracy which it would take to make it happen. The French and the Dutch said "no thanks," and this meant the Constitution was dead. The scheduled British ballot never came to pass.

This came as a bit of a blow to Prime Minister Tony Blair. He had faithfully promised the people of Great Britain that they would get to have a referendum on the proposed EU Constitution and so he was frustrated when the French and Dutch nay sayers made further balloting irrelevant. Tony's frustration was based in his absolute belief that the Brits would cheerfully affirm this overwhelmingly complex EU plan to run their lives. He wanted the Euro-skeptics (people who think that the EU is an anti-British conspiracy) to be silenced once and for all. Talk about not knowing the lay of the land.

Now let's fast-forward a bit to the present. Fresh from the worst days - so far - of his brief Prime Ministership, Gordon Brown flew off to Lisbon late last week. That is where the somewhat new cast of characters who now run the 27 EU member states were meeting to plot a sales campaign. Their goal was to get people to buy into the "new" EU Constitution that has now been repackaged as a "Reform Treaty." The thing is, by all accounts from everyone who has read it, the "new" Treaty consists of 90 percent of the "old" and rejected, EU Constitution, with the added ten percent being even more power-grabbing.

Regular readers may recall reading here recently that Gordon Brown wants like anything to distance himself from Tony Blair, the man and the track record, despite the fact that Brown was running his fair share of the New Labour shop during the Blair decade. So what is he do in this case?

Since Tony Blair had promised the people of Britain unequivocally that they would get to vote on accepting the EU Constitution because they deserved to have a say in their own national sovereignty, this left Brown to take the opposite position. He declared that there would be no referendum on this new Treaty, which he signed on the dotted line. To assuage their concerns, Brown assured the people that he had won agreements from his EU comrades by "red lining" aspects of the new Treaty's rules and regulations. These opt-out provisions would be sacrosanct and would not be applicable on English soil, at least for now, and for maybe as long as ten years, Brown promised. These opt outs include foreign policy and justice issues, two major components of any country's identity.

Brown had given the Tories another battle cry. The week before, he had unilaterally decided not to give the British populace a chance to vote him his own mandate to be their Prime Minister, and now he was telling them they would not be allowed to vote on their national right to remain free of a power hungry EU bureaucracy. In Gordon Brown, the British people had found a man who was truly ballot phobic.

For a second time in as many weeks, Tory leader David Cameron rushed to the media outlets to declare that, without a referendum, any Treaty which Brown signed on behalf of the nation would be democratically illegitimate. But as usual when pressed, the Conservatives seemed unclear on what exactly they might do if the Treaty was affirmed by the present, Labour dominated, Parliament and was also ratified across Europe. Decisions are always tricky when one has mislaid one's basic philosophical principles and cojones are in short supply.

But just when you think that a story has run its course, the running backs of irony pick up the ball and run it a bit further down the field. Much has been made of the fact that Gordon Brown hails from Scotland, a country which is now flexing its own muscles and hinting that it wants to leave the auspices of the United Kingdom. This movement toward full independence has emerged after years of a process known as devolution, a plan put in place by the Labour Party. Little by little, Scotland has been given the power to manage its own internal affairs and elect its own government to make things happen. Now, there is talk that the Scots will be offered the option of a referendum in which they get to vote on complete sovereignty. The paradox is hard to ignore.

So, much to the continuing chagrin of Gordon Brown, is the ubiquitous Tony Blair. Over the post-Lisbon weekend, the newspapers were full of leaks about a forthcoming book by Britain's leading political biographer, Anthony Seldon. The book focuses on the hostile relationship between PM Blair and his former Chancellor (Treasury Secretary) Brown. Seldon recounts that after one very rude verbal attack on Blair, by Brown loyalist Ed Balls, poor old Tony is said to have exclaimed: "I feel like an abused and bullied wife."

One could hear the titters all over town. But the handwriting on the wall is unmistakable. Blair and Co. are determined to undermine Gordon Brown, as if he needed their help to do that.

The second shoe was dropped in the Monday morning European rumor mill. The idea of Tony Blair becoming the first full time, non-rotating, President of the European Union resurfaced. This made news several months back when the newly elected French President Sarkozy first floated the idea publicly. Once Tony Blair does his thing in the Middle East and finishes his memoir (for which he got a multi million dollar advance thanks to Bill Clinton's book agent), how could he refuse an appointed (not elective) position with far-reaching perks and power?

Will the British ever get to have their EU Treaty referendum? That question remains unanswered unless and until the Tories find the courage to make a do or die stand. If they fail to win the day, the British people will clearly lose what is left of their heritage and their dignity.

October 23, 2007

Ships and Trains of State

On Tuesday November 6th, Queen Elizabeth earned her pay packet. She appeared at the Opening of Parliament in the morning and cut the metaphorical ribbon for the fabulously-refurbished Saint Pancras train station in the evening.

The first of these two events is required by British tradition. When Parliament reconvenes, the Queen (or King) must appear, in full royal regalia, to read an address written by the government in power. It is a de facto set of campaign promises. Elizabeth II has done this for all 10 prime ministers before Gordon Brown and now she's reading his political script. It did not go without notice by the British press that this time her Majesty read through the statement very quickly, as if she wanted to be done in record time or had an imminent hair dressing appointment.

There were 28 items put forth in the Brown program which the Prime Minster characterized as an agenda designed to respond to the rising aspirations of the British people. Rising ways of collecting taxes is more like it. There's the "throw as you go" trash collection fee plan and new road pricing - toll and congestion charging - schemes. The cost to British taxpayers for these grand plans has yet to be calculated. The cost of the makeover of Saint Pancras station was 800 million quid ($1.68 billion) when it was done and dusted. One caller to a Radio Five talk show said that the new Saint Pancras station was of bloody little use to him as it took him four hours to get into London by domestic train and he didn't want to go to Paris or Brussels anyway and he would have preferred that his taxes were put to more practical use. Who can blame him for being a touch grouchy?

While a quick trip to Paris or Brussels on the 186 mile per hour Eurostar, 20 minutes of it underwater, is being touted as a benchmark of modern civilization, Britain has otherwise been sucked into a societal bog with unfathomable depths. The Brown legislative proposals, so hastily read by her Madge, are a litany of what the Labour government under Blair and Brown had already promised and never fulfilled after a decade in power.

Here are a few more items on Gordon Brown's wish list.

There are requests for new monies to be thrown after bad in the areas of education, housing, and the health service. One Brown initiative wants to deliver more than three million new homes by 2020. There are also proposals to fast-track new nuclear installations, motorways, and airports. The protestors are, of course, already slapping paint on the signs to lobby against all of these environmental transgressions. The "not in my backyard" fervor runs high among the eccentric people of this island nation.

And here is a bit of oxymoronic imagining. Brown's government wants to build dozens of "zero carbon eco-towns," (trademark pending) each with between 5,000 and 20,000 affordable homes, but with all the supermarkets sited on the town perimeters where you'd have to drive to get your food. Hello? And where would these eco town residents work? Hardly in the countryside where cattle are continually culled because of disease and the trains into London are not dependable. Another Radio Five caller described train schedules as the most widely read category of fiction in Britain. There is a noticeable absence of entrepreneurial incentives in any of these Brown (or is that green) visions, but one expects little more from a socialist.

Now to school. There are an estimated 450,000 children in British primary schools who do not speak English as their first language. Drop out rates are high across the educational spectrum including 40 percent at the university level. Thus, Mr. Brown has pledged to raise the age when it is legal to leave the educational system. You must now be 18 to drop out, not to be confused with when you can drink or have sex. How will this be policed? No word. Furthermore, local authorities will be expected to "help" all unmarried teenager mothers go back to school as soon as possible after having their babies. Is this to be accomplished via a vast government babysitting plan? Who knows? In a related move, Brown wants all employees to be free to request flexible working hours to look after their children. You've spotted the organizational nightmare, yes?

Another proposed bill would give MPs a greater say in sending troops overseas and would transfer the Intelligence and Security Committee out of Downing Street's control. One supposes this will prevent any future Prime Ministers from being blamed for bad intelligence – like Tony Blair has been over proferring "sexed up" reports about WMD's. Terrorists, especially suicide bombers, are no doubt seriously considering the implications of Brown's desire to extend the current 28 day limit on detaining terror suspects without charging them. Or their remaining body parts.

The Queen's speech also contained Brown's assurance that the NHS (national health service) would, in future, be organized around the needs of the patient and that legislation would be passed to ensure "clean and safe services and high-quality care." This would be funny if so many people weren't dead or dying from the current system's ministrations. Brits are so desperately unhappy with their collapsing socialist heath care system that they are reportedly pulling their own teeth rather than wait forever to get a dental appointment. NHS hospitals are breeding grounds for superbugs. One is more likely to die from unwashed hands than any disease.

And so it goes.

After the Queen's speech, the members of Parliament met to debate. To the surprise of many, Tory leader David Cameron pulled no punches. He excoriated Gordon Brown and insulted him by saying that at least Tony Blair was consistent. Ouch. The opinion polls indicate that Cameron is gathering support by attacking Brown with such ferocity. With the financial sector becoming increasingly jumpy, the Tories have Labour on the defensive.

Brown is clinging to the hope that his wish list of legislative ideas will help revive his poll numbers. As if. According to a reliable poll, the number of people who believe Brown will prove a good Prime Minister has, in a single month, dropped five points to 49 per cent. This is ten points below his midsummer peak approval rating. Perhaps more wounding to the crusty Scot, the number of those who believe he is even "likeable" has dropped to 44 percent, a nine point decline since late July.

There is no figure on the number of Brits who are thoroughly ticked off over Brown's refusal to allow them to vote the EU "Reform Treaty" off the Island. When reality TV offers more electoral options than your Prime Minister does, things are out of kilter. That's a Scottish joke.

A recent episode of the UK comedy current events program, "Have I Got News For You," showed a rodent running past the front door of Number 10 Downing Street. The gag line was: "evidence of the first rat ever to jump on a sinking ship." Clever that.

November 8, 2007

British Religious Leader Provides Anti-American Words for Muslim Magazine

Rowan Williams has wildly uncultivated eyebrows. They would appear to be a visual representation of his increasingly unkempt political sensibilities. How else can one account for the fact that the sitting Archbishop of Canterbury (aka the ABC) just delivered a vociferously anti-American diatribe via an exclusive interview in the Muslim magazine, Emel?

For those who need a quick point of reference, the Archbishop of Canterbury is the ecclesiastical head (primate) of the Church of England, and the world-wide Anglican Communion, comprising 80 million members, including the Episcopal Church in America. He is a Pope-like figure whose control over his flock is in turmoil at the moment. The reigning monarch -- Queen Elizabeth II -- is the titular head of the Church of England. This has to do with Henry VIII's break from Rome and the real meaning of an established religion.

The focus here is why the spiritual leader of a global church felt compelled to give political ammo to any Islamic organization in these perilous times. One ought first to consider the source of the interview.

Emel is a lifestyle magazine, the Muslim equivalent of "People."

The interview itself was conducted in the ABC's office in Lambeth Palace, very lavish as opposed to monastic digs, just across the Thames from the Houses of Parliament. The reporter sent to conduct the interview was a young female given to describing the ABC's voice as essentially ethereal and his comments as being delivered in a state of "serene tranquility." One needs only to close a single eye to set the scene.

The furor erupted when ABC Williams remarked on how the US had lost the high moral ground since 9-11. The interview prompted the Times of London to report the interview under the headline: "US is Worst Imperalist."

What Williams specifically said about US foreign policy was: "It is one thing to take over a territory and then pour energy and resources into administering it and normalizing it. Rightly or wrongly, that's was the British empire did -- in India, for example. It is another thing to go in on the assumption that a quick burst of violent action will somehow clear the decks and that you can move on and other people will put things back together -- Iraq, for example."

The ABC's position on such matters is hardly news. He has been an outspoken critic of the war in Iraq from the get-go. In the Emel interview he spoke of how the invasion of Iraq might have been "a quick discharge of frustration," but he added, "It serves you. It does not serve the situation." In other words, the US invasion of Iraq was a feel good exercise which has now, by virtue of US exploitation, left a country in ruins, both on the civil and economic levels. Fair enough, some might say. Religious figures tend to be anti-war. Trouble was -- at no time did he mention that the Tube and bus bombing of July 7 2005, in London, might easily be described as a similar discharge of easy anger. To ABC Williams, there's no need to condemn terrorism, only Americans.

But beyond the superficial quotes, there are both historical and spiritual cracks which run deep, and not so silently, beneath the pseudo-noble surface of the ABC's remarks. Comparing modern America's foreign policy to the height of the British Empire's sins of omission and commission toward its colonies is an antihistorical enterprise. It is apples and oranges. The proof of this position is that Williams went on to suggest that America ought to purge its foreign policy sins by engaging in a "generous and intelligent program of aid directed to the societies that have been ravaged." This statement belies an ignorance of the vast sums of foreign aid dispensed by the US to nations across the globe.

The controversy was further fueled when, coincidently, former US Ambassador to the United Nations John Bolton was to appear on BCC's Radio Four on Sunday, to plug his new book, which urges the US to attack Iran. Bolton's radio spot was scheduled as a one-off, with no one who held opposing views on hand to debate his ideas. Bolton took advantage of the opportunity to lambaste the resident primate of Lambeth Palace for not concentrating on his day job and, instead, venturing into areas outside his area of expertise.

The Rev. Dr. Peter Mullen, Rector of Saint Michael's Cornhill in London and Chaplain to the London Stock Exchange, is a noted and prolific conservative critic of the present-day state of affairs in the Anglican Communion. He has crossed theological swords with Archbishop Williams on many occasions and this is no exception.

About this specific interview Mullen responds: "Christians are being beaten up, robbed, illegally imprisoned -- their churches burnt to the ground -- in Muslim countries all over the world," exclaims Mullen, "yet all Williams can do is return to his leftie America-bashing. He ought to be ashamed of himself."

Indeed, there are sheep in Williams' pasture who could benefit from his attention. Consider the situation facing the British teacher presently facing 40 lashes from a Sharia court in Sudan. Gillian Gibbons, a 54-year-old woman who gave up her teaching job in Liverpool three months ago to teach in the Sudan, has been accused of insulting Islam by allowing a child in her class to name a teddy bear "Mohamed." Perhaps Williams' energy might be better spent trying to save Gibbons than condemning America.

November 29, 2007

Global Wallet Warming

On his way to pick up his Nobel Prize, Algore stopped off in London to deliver an address to The Fortune Forum. His back-up group of global warmies included The Prince of Brunei, Bob Geldorf, David Frost, Darryl Hannah and Jerry Hall (the ex Mrs. Mick Jagger).

In case the name of the host organization glanced too lightly off your intellectual windscreen, go back one sentence and read the name of Algore's hosts. They are "The Fortune Forum," a self-proclaimed multi-issue global group devoted to the red-hot issues of the day. This includes fighting poverty.

The Fortune Forum does appear to live up to its title. In 2006, Bill Clinton became the highest paid public speaker in the world when he made three speeches. When combined, the fees for these three talks helped him pay off his legal fees and buy the Clinton homes in both Chappaqua, NY, and Georgetown, D.C. One of these speeches was to help launch the Fortune Forum Summit in London for that year. His cohort for the evening was Mr. "Greed is Good," Michael Douglas. Tickets for that FF event were 1,000 pounds a head or about $1850 at the 2006 pound to dollar conversion rate.

We shall now defer to the Fortune Forum website for an explanation of the scope of global poverty:

"More then 1 billion people still live below the extreme poverty line of $1 a day, and 20,000 die from poverty each day. More then 3 billion, more then half of humanity, live in poverty, with less then $2 per day. Over 1 billion people have no access to health care. Out of the population of the developing countries 66% have no toilets, nor even latrines."

But those are mere statistics. At The Fortune Forum in late November of 07, money was no object. (This is an attempt at irony). The audience included world leaders, entrepreneurs and (surprise) celebrity activists, who, when they could bend their minds to think about things other than whose designer clothing label they were wearing, were in heated anticipation of Algore's speech. They ought to have had great expectations. The price tag to attend this gala poverty consciousness-raising event was as high as $100,000 per person. Lesser fees were probably (if at all) paid by those whose names are aforementioned.

According to reliable sources, Saint Al was his usual humble self when he arrived to give his speech to The Fortune Forum. Of course, he insisted on a VIP room for himself and his entourage, barring any and all press from his presence. The better to be holy.

Who bought into the evening? Scan the official website and you will see photos of both Tony Blair and Gordon Brown making warm welcoming remarks to the well-heeled guests. Then check out the photos of the glitterati -- all arriving in haute couture evening wear. Say, isn't that Sir David Frost who left the BCC for the Al Jazerra TV Network? There's Cat Stevens, the American pop songwriter who converted to Islam. Isn't that Darryl Hannah who slept at least once with JFK Jr. and can hold her breath long enough to portray a believable mermaid?

The most credible Fortune Forum guest might well have been a woman who was once married to an aging rock star. Yes, the ex Mrs. Mick Jagger. Bless him, Mick knew how to stash his cash before he made it because he has a degree from The London School of Economics. Lest we get us a fatwa, one does not dare remark on the fabulously wealthy Prince of Brunei, nor on the blond arm candy which adorns him. Eat your heart out, Paris Hilton.

Did we mention the location of the poverty consciousness raising dinner?? That would be THE ROYAL COURTS OF JUSTICE. Yes, you can apparently BUY Justice -- or at least eat there in London -- for the right price.

What's the punchline? Apparently, when Algore rose to the podium he delivered a speech that was SO boring that guests reportedly began talking among themselves before it was over. Other Fortune Forum members subsequently trashed the speech in press interviews. Well, boo. What did they expect for a mere $200,000 (or -- as it worked out on the clock -- $6,600 per minute)?

Worse yet, some of the charities that were to benefit from this fund raising event were treated (gasp) like "uninvited guests." They did not get to meet the Nobel Gore whose causes he was there to triumph. Fortune Forum organizers apologized to some of the other invited guests when they expressed dismay over their inability to have a photo taken with Al. In England they call this "a shambles."

A spokesperson for the expert on hot air later made it clear that Mr. Gore was donating "a percentage of his fees" to the Alliance for Climate Protection.

Go to the website and start by taking the pledge. Once that's done, click on "At The Store" and there you will find a variety of ways to purge your climate guilt by further thinning out your own wallet. Like with a line of vintage clothing.

Al Gore is in that business in case you couldn't guess. It is The Global Warming Shell Game. Players are simply being suckered into padding Al Gore's warmed up wallet. Gore is, need we say it, very hot.

November 12, 2007

The EU's Treaty Treachery

To millions of Britons, December 13, 2007 is a date which will live in infamy.

In the Labor Party's 2006 Election Manifesto, the British people were given a devout promise that there would be a referendum on whether to sign on to the proposed EU Constitution. Gordon Brown reaffirmed this vow when he succeeded Tony Blair as Prime Minister in July of this year. The promise was an empty one. The proposed EU Constitution -- meant to replace all previous treaties -- was already legally dead thanks to "no" votes by both the French and the Dutch in 2005.

But behind the scenes, there has been treachery afoot these past 30 months. Bureaucrats never take your "no" for the answer to what they want. Slowly, the Euro forces began cosmetic surgery. The Constitution underwent a political makeover and re-emerged as the new EU Reform Treaty, a document which is not only the same as the failed EU Constitution, but has added even more bureaucracy to it.

On Thursday morning, December 13 in Lisbon, Portugal, the Presidents and Prime Ministers from the 27 member nations were to gather to sign this new Treaty. All were present except for Gordon Brown. He sent his Foreign Minister. David Milliband signed this historical document on behalf of the UK when the cameras were flashing. Brown explained his absence as a "conflict of scheduling." Then events took a turn toward treachery worthy of a Shakespearian play. Three hours later, Brown surreptitiously arrived. Cowering in a back room off the main hall - where he had hoped in vain to avoid the cameras -- the pusillanimous Prime Minister signed the document. One EU insider dryly remarked that Brown acted like someone who was trying to keep a dirty little secret.

Brown seems to have imagined that this out-of-sight out-of-mind tactic would fool the British public. Hardly. The Shadow (Conservative) Foreign Minister, William Hague, asked what the members of the EU would think of a man who "dithers for a week about whether or not he wants to be photographed putting pen to paper." To others it was more a case of Brown proving to be as handy with a knife as Brutus.

So just what are the most important points of the so-called "Reform Treaty" as they impact minor details like, for instance, British sovereignty?

The EU is designed to be a superstructure entity that creates a single foreign policy and one-stop overarching decision-making powers which will be directed downwards to all its member states. Until now, the heads of the 27 member nations served six month rotations as nominal EU President. That egalitarian practice is now dead. There is to be a new all-powerful unelected President of Europe, appointed by the 27 heads of state - not elected by the 350 million people of new Europe. (Frustrated Democrats who have never gotten over the US 2000 election, please note). Tony Blair, former Prime Minister of the UK, has been heavily tipped to take over this coveted post.

Although the initial idea of a single EU Foreign Minister was abandoned in this round of "ever closer union", the new Treaty calls for a Foreign Policy Chief -- who will hold diplomatic status and head up the new EU Foreign Service bureaucracy. What's in a name? Perhaps everything.

Great Britain and Poland asked to opt out of signing on to the 50-article Charter of Fundamental Rights -- for the time being. This charter promises life, liberty, the pursuit of happiness, and religions freedom. It then goes on to promise universal collective bargaining, fair working conditions and shelter. Yes, shelter. No one in the New Europe will be allowed to be homeless.

The UK continues to demure on joining the Euro. But this Treaty puts yet more pressure on Great Britain to ditch the Pound in favor of New Europe's collective currency.

The most sinister part of the Treaty is contained in another rule. This one gives the EU rights to overturn decisions made by Britain's Immigration and Asylum Tribunal. Those who have sought -- and have been rejected -- as asylum seekers in the UK now have the right to take their cases over the head of Great Britain's highest court and appeal to the unelected European Court of Justice in Luxembourg whose EU bureaucrats will have the final say. Giving the EU authorities power to trump immigration and border issues inside the UK is seen as the end of their democracy by many a Brit. When the EU Court of Justice can overrule any member nation's own judiciary, another piece of national sovereignty has been signed away.

The output of venom directed against the Prime Minister since Wednesday's dirty deed has been stunning. The most vociferous critics of Brown's stealth execution of the treaty are calling for his severed head to be skewered on a pike and set above the Thames. This was often the fate of traitors in earlier times. The British have such colorful traditions. Others have suggested that the Tower of London be re-commissioned to serve as a prison for Brown and his minions. Calls have been raised for a million people to surround the Houses of Parliament in a massive protest where this Treaty must be ratified in the House of Commons. Two full weeks of debate have been promised the public -- but then promises come cheap in politics.

Brown himself has been compared to Neville Chamberlain, who returned to England from Germany in 1938 waving a paper which Adolph Hitler had written promising that there would be no future war. British veterans and their heirs must surely wonder why two world wars were fought and millions of lives lost if the British sovereignty would eventually be surrendered -- by their own government -- to their former continental enemies. Brown is also now being parodied in cartoons and editorials which compare him to that bumbling silent English loner, Mr. Bean. After all, the wags point out, Brown doesn't like to even mingle with his EU counterparts. Brown bungles about like Mr. Bean, although Mr. Bean's awkwardness and its consequences are inadvertent. And like the bumbling Mr. Bean, since Brown went slinking off to Portugal to sign away his country's autonomy, Brown has mumbled to the English press that the new EU treaty "would provide a lasting framwork for the EU" yet at the same time create "a circle of reflection" on the EU's long term future.

Of course, there is a technical flaw in that observation. Gordon Brown isn't English. He's a sly and canny Scot. Come to that, so is Tony Blair. Many a wary English eye is now being cast north of Hadrian's Wall. Just a few months ago, the ever more powerful Scottish Parliament voted to give every one of its citizens free health care, the costs for which will be taken out of English pockets. Is the new Europe Reform Treaty part of the Great Scottish Plot? Is this Braveheart's Revenge?

December 17, 2009

Remembering 2007 in News

There are 25 stories in my 2007 HUMAN EVENTS archive. As the year wound down it seemed appropriate to revisit them, thus avoiding the media contagion known as Disposable News Disorder.

Christopher Hitchens' book, "God is Not Great," was one of the 150 top selling books of 07. He has since produced another -- "The Portable Atheist," just in time for the Christmas gift market. Hitchens practiced a form of self-mortification when he invited Vanity Fair magazine to give him a makeover. The photos of his scotch-saturated and tobacco-tainted teeth made many a reader exclaim: "Good God."

For a second time, a book by Richard Dawkins (the first being "The Selfish Gene") crossed the line between literature and politics. Despite the movement to grant Turkey admittance to the European Union as a presumed secular state, the Turkish publisher of Dawkins' "The God Delusion" was threatened with legal action (or worse) for printing ideas which are insulting to the Islamic faith.

In mid-December, the Pope got an early Christmas present when Tony Blair officially converted to the Catholic faith. Blair claimed he hadn't done it sooner lest people think he was "a nutter." Many replied: "Too late Tony." Blair is serving now as a negotiator in the Middle East peace process. The Pope is not a popular figure in the Islamic world which begs the question -- how will Tony's road to Damascus conversion be viewed by Muslims? By the Israelis? Quite honestly, the prospects for peace on earth look dim when one reads that -- two days after the Christmas pilgrims departed -- Greek Orthodox and Armenian priests brawled over how to clean up the Church of the Nativity in Bethlehem.

Another dust up in UK politics is on the horizon. Gordon Brown is facing a bonafide insurrection. A sufficient number of his own Labour Party members have promised to vote NO on Brown's request to hold terror suspects for up to 42 days without charging them. The current holding time is 28 days. Those against the extension say the system is not broken and needs no fixing on the basis of hypothetical cases. Brown has appointed a "fixer" to save himself from a public drubbing.

Behind this battle is the feeling that Brown's holding time as PM needs to be shortened. Stories are now leaking about Labour's secreted mini-revolts, staged against Brown from the get-go. The party of a sitting Prime Minister can call, at any time, for a vote of no confidence. That usually means a general election is soon to follow. This fall, the Labour government confessed it had lost two major data bases full of private details -- financial and otherwise -- on British citizens. We're talking a great many British citizens. This has thrust the otherwise lackluster Tories ahead in the polls. But does anyone really want to run this island loony bin?

How crazy is the UK government's decision to require the National Health Service (NHS) to cover surgical procedures for Muslim women who wish to regain their virginity (a must have for one's wedding night)? From 2005-06, there were 24 taxpayer funded hymen replacements. Muslim women who do not want to "go public" pay up to £4,000 (roughly $8K US) to have their virginity restored in private clinics. Medical science meets hypocrisy!

Other UK '07 firsts -- on the Islamic feminist front -- include the conviction of a Muslim woman for engaging in terrorist activities. This legal decision coincided with a two-part Channel Four TV program. In BRITZ, the daughter of a Muslim family decides to join the jihad after her friends are hassled by police. Her commitment to the cause begins with wearing a hijab (head scarf).

In real life news, a hijab-wearing hair stylist sued the owner of a British beauty salon over job discrimination. The salon specializes in offering "urban funky" cuts and the owner said she wanted employees who would model these hairstyles to the public.

The suit demands that the salon owner -- who is now the target of racist taunts and threats -- pay the plaintiff more than the business earns in a year. Jihad against gels? You be the judge.

In the mixed fortunes department, the twin Kaczyñski brothers, who were serving together as President and Prime Minister of Poland, had their family act broken up by voters. The new Prime Minister, Donald Tusk, delivered his first policy speech to the lower chamber of Parliament on November 23. It was standing room only except for the chair left empty by President Lech Kaczyñski. Lech went on a state visit to Georgia rather than listen to the man who beat his bro.

The Polish press reported that the President's absence was not the only unusual element of the day. The new Prime Minister rocked the house by delivering a stirring message about people's freedoms, including the freedom to be economically active and to make money. Private ownership -- on which true freedom rests -- is something the Kaczynski Brothers kept limited to an absolute minimum. In fact, the former Prime Minister, Jaros[3]aw Kaczyñski, once said that there was no room in Poland for the rich.

Meanwhile, the President of France has caused the tabloids to go on steroids to keep up with his love life. After a lightening fast divorce from his wife of 11 years, Nicholas Sarkozy added a series of high profile dates with glamorous women to his already mind-boggling schedule of diplomatic forays across Europe and beyond. There is so little romance in today's headlines.

Speaking of which, the British press has penned more articles on Hillary Clinton. Several focus on how her sham marriage to Bill could be what keeps her out of The White House. If journalists decide to dog old Billy and uncover the details of his current love life, US voters could decide to cancel this soap opera rather than renew the series for another four to eight year run.

The prize for extending one's own political life in 2007 goes to Vladimir Putin. After choosing his successor, Dmitry Medvedev, Putin volunteered to become Medvedev's Prime Minister after he, Putin, steps down as President next year. (He cannot legally try for a third term at this time). He has urged the government to smooth the path for his career transition. As if there would be resistance. A week ago, it was revealed that Putin, during his eight years in office, may have stashed away a personal fortune in the $40 billion range. Far from being a cold-hearted tycoon, Vlad just ask if someone could give his dog a GPS chip in case he wanders off. Nor does Putin abandon a human friend in need. Repeated attempts by the British government to extradite Andrei Lugovoi for the fatal poisoning of fellow former KGB agent -- and anti-Putin activist -- Alexander Litvinenko, (in Nov. 2006) have been rebuffed by the Kremlin. Andrei Lugovoi is now not only a multi-millionaire member of Russia's economic oligarchy, he is running for political office with Putin's blessings.

As these words hit the keyboard, Pakistan is in turmoil. Iowa (and the rest of the US electoral process) now looks like an exercise in self-absorbed inanity. The only thing more alight than Karachi -- as the year comes to a close -- is the Draft Al Gore movement on the Internet.

A personal note: To all those who have read my reports -- and especially to those who took the time to comment (either way) -- Thanks and Happy New Year!

December 31, 2007

Iowa from Across the Pond

British media reports on the Iowa Caucuses could have been written by anthropologist Margaret Mead. Well, perhaps not. She's dead. Attempts to explain the caucus process often sounded similar to descriptions of an island tribe that eats funny mushrooms and then conducts mysterious rituals in order to select a new chieftain.

As outside (albeit not always unbiased) observers, British and European reporters, editorialists, and bloggers offered any number of nuanced assessments of what had happened in Iowa and what it suggested about America's immediate political future.

Three distinct ideas emerged.

For a start, the press agreed that the aloof and arrogant Mrs. Clinton had gotten her nose bloodied. A post caucus photo of Hillary - looking quizzical and perplexed - became instantly iconic. Much was made of boos and groans emitted from the crowds she was trolling for support. A reporter from The Independent somewhat gleefully wrote that Hillary had, "been forced to drink from the bitter cup of defeat." Another journalist opined that a third place finish in Iowa was a good thing for Hillary because it placed her in the position of being an underdog as opposed to being seen as the ultimate ice queen. Perhaps so, and what a frightening thought -- Hillary unleashed. It was as if, one wag asserted, Hillary had shot Bambi and was being shunned. Comeuppance makes for jolly good copy.

The extent of her Party's rejection of Hillary was dead simple math. The majority of Iowa's caucusing Democrats had pledged their allegiance to either Obama or Edwards. This put paid to the notion that Hillary had a lock on the Party ticket. The shift away from Hillary was personified by old Clintonian team member, Bill

Richardson. It was whispered that he had encouraged his limited number of supporters to throw in their lot with Obama because Richardson could more comfortably see himself as the first Hispanic running mate for the first Black -- male -- candidate for the Presidency. (Richardson's Mother was Mexican). This line of thought concluded -- not so subtly -- with the notion that Hillary's reputation as a ball-busting harridan would make any male running mate tense.

The Independent on Sunday reported that Obama-mania had spread like wildfire into New Hampshire and predicted Mrs. Clinton "faced a mincing" at the polls on Tuesday. David Usborne's article also noted the irony of hearing a mixed demographic crowd shouting "O BA MA," in the state which was the last to adopt the Martin Luther King holiday.

The second set of observations were all quizzes: what about Obama? The short answer is that he is now the man to beat. Self proclaimed conservative commentator, Andrew Sullivan, writing for The Sunday Times, listed all the cliché Obama analogies (rock star, cult leader, new JFK but more like Bobby) then made a bold leap by suggesting that Obama could become a liberal version of Ronald Reagan. That is to say, Reagan won the Presidency by gaining a following among disaffected Democrats and now Obama could do likewise by attracting support from disaffected Republicans. Sullivan goes on to claim that Obama could even become "the Thatcher of the left," which might be just a bit over the top and would require skill sets usually found only among circus contortionists. But it is not impossible and that's the point. The dream.

But leave it to The Daily Mail to make a personal tabloid-style connection. Mail reporter, Elizabeth Sanderson went to the wilds of Bracknell (in the Berkshires) and got an exclusive interview with -- wait for it -- Obama's stepmother, Kezia. Now 67, Kezia was the first of the Senior Barack's three wives. They married when he was (according to her) a modest Muslim goat herder in Kenya. There were three sons from that marriage. When the Senior Obama got a scholarship to the US, he met Obama Junior's Mother and at this point the family history gets a bit confusing because it appears that the Senior Obama's third marriage to a woman named Ruth made him a bigamist.

The bottom line of the interview with Kezia is that Barack Junior takes all his family obligations seriously, is well mannered, affectionate, has read a lot of history books, and looks and sounds a great deal like his Dad. Here's the interesting bit. The article was highlighted in a box on the front page of the Daily's Sunday edition, but by early evening London time, it had been taken down and buried in the paper's archives. Even for our press, that's a suspicious turn of events.

This brings us to the final tier of overseas observations, the socio-political trend spotting. Several pundits assessed Iowa as being the harbinger of a new American populist revival. By voting for Huckabee and Obama, Iowans had rejected the status quo. This led Leonard Doyle of the Independent to describe the Iowa results as "a polite insurgency."

Indeed, the BCC informed the British public, this American election is quite unique. It is the first time in half a century that neither a sitting President, nor a serving Vice President, is up for election or re-election - a perfect point for a change in direction.

"The Huckabama Phenomenon" as one journalist tagged it, is seen as an expression of America's need for a renewal of values and spirit. This accounted for the victories of man who once was a preacher and the other whose charismatic speeches are continually compared to those of Dr. King. This makes European secularists nervous.

But Sam Leith, writing in the UK Telegraph, notes that although America's religiosity puts some people off, it indicates the robust structure which girds the country. Leith posits that America maintains enough of a common identity for the people to know what they want and to go out and get it. Americans, Leith asserts, do not simply have fervor about political creeds. They are still true believers in the system itself.

Who will win the Presidency in November? Cynics fret and grumble about how no politician can be trusted. But the odds in the betting parlours are that Americans will elect that person who best embodies America's national faith in itself -- the one who can stir up visions for a better day ahead. As it says in the Bible: "Without a vision, the people perish."

January 7, 2008

Gordon Brown Wants Your Organs

The UK Nanny State just revealed its latest agenda item and it is decidedly ghoulish. Last week, British (but really Scottish) Prime Minister, Gordon Brown, announced his support of a Labour government plan to snatch the body parts of any citizen. The good news is that this policy only applies to dead people. The bad news is obvious. This is the ultimate death tax, surgically extracted.

Without any apparent squeamishness, Gordon Brown backed the Presumed Consent Scheme (they often call programs "schemes" in England) to redress the demand for transplanted organs by fiat. Here's the deal. Rather than go looking for those bothersome donor cards on a fresh cadaver, the British populace is now fair game. If you don't specifically carry a card saying "leave my corpse alone" -- known as "the opt out option", or unless one's family is on hand to object, one's remains are considered fair game for an organ harvest festival.

The justification for adopting Presumed Consent is a function of a recognized market deficit. The Government has noticed that 1000 patients die annually while waiting for a critically-needed transplant. Another 8000 are on various organ waiting lists hoping to get lucky when they go critical or for just the right replacement part to turn up in the chop shop.

According to the NHS Organ Donor Registry, there are more than 14 million Brits who have voluntarily listed themselves as donors, however, one third of all families refuse consent for organ donation when a loved one dies, usually in unexpected circumstances. In typical fashion, the government plans to overcome this donor reluctance by setting up -- you guessed it -- a new Task Force to enlighten the populace about the importance of giving this gift of life.

But the reality is that Gordon Brown is not pushing this policy to engender a national altruistic ethos. Truth to tell, this PC (and you can't overlook those initials) scheme has more to do with failures in both the National Health System (NHS) and the just plain horrid health of UK citizens.

For a start, going to the hospital in the UK can kill you. The number of patient deaths in NHS hospitals from the super bug MRSA (Methicillin Resistant Staphylococcus Aureus) continues to rise. MRSA bacteria are commonly found on the skin and are difficult to treat with conventional antibiotics. MRSA is spread when medical personnel and the hospital cleaning staff do not wash their hands properly. The actual number of MRSA deaths are impossible to count since the super bug is rarely the primary cause of death, but up to 1000 deaths per year is a good guess. That's the same number as those who die annually waiting for a transplant. Likewise, in 2007, 3,663 cases of Pseudomonas were reported in British hospitals, a 41% rise over 2006. Pseudomonas bacteria - commonly known as septicemia or blood poisoning - breed in water and spread via contaminated medical equipment. Patients who contract pseudomonas have a 20 per cent chance of survival. Those who do not die outright can suffer blindness or the loss of limbs.

In an attempt to stop the spread of these modern day plagues, the NHS spent an estimated £1,000,000,000 (that's roughly $2 billion) in 2007. And as long as we're talking about real money, NHS hospitals have run up debts of £1 billion, creating a critical health care credit crunch. The UK Telegraph claims that more than 20 percent of NHS hospital trusts "are so dependent on loans to meet their running costs that millions of pounds intended for patient care are due to be diverted to pay debts and interest payments." 55 hospital trusts are known to have loans totaling close to £800 million, with interest payments nearing the £200 million mark. To pay these loans and the interest, medical staff and services, already substandard, will have to be cut. The Labour government continues to insist that the NHS is NOT facing a financial crisis. One wonders by what measure a pending medical system meltdown would be acknowledged.

Here is the donor dilemma. If one enters a hospital for kidney dialysis and contracts an MRSA, dialysis can no longer be performed. But even if a donor organ is found, there is no guarantee the recipient will be isolated from MRSA. Intensive Care Units are equally vulnerable to MRSA outbreaks.

To escape the NHS, more than 70,000 Britons -- known as "health tourists" -- have gone as far as India, Malaysia and South Africa for major operations. This figure is expected to rise to almost 200,000 by the end of the decade.

Enter the EU twist. A Health Services Directive is before the European Union. It would guarantee that patients from any EU member nation would be entitled to treatment in every other member nation "with no worry about costs, safety and quality." Perhaps this is why Gordon Brown was torn about signing the New EU Reform Treaty a few months back. He wanted to be in the club, but he also knows that an influx of immigrants and visitors seeking health care in the UK could bring about the complete collapse of the NHS. This is not a happy legacy.

Those in favor of Presumed Consent say that what is done with their organs after death should not be up to their next of kin, which frankly misses the point. A voluntary donor system already exists. The naysayers come down against this idea on the basis that there will always be a bungling bureaucrat who will invariably screw up the paperwork (or hack off the wrong part). More importantly, freedom lovers assert that totalitarianism cannot be disguised as humanitarianism.

One blogger ironically suggested that Presumed Consent would have the greatest appeal to the British tax authorities. A number of transplant patients will defy the odds and be able to resume productive working lives. Once they begin to earn taxable income again, these additional revenues will go into the bottomless pit of Labour schemes and to fight the war against super bugs.

To bolster his position on Presumed Consent, Brown cited the "success" of this policy in Spain which, inarguably, has the highest organ donor rate in the world. This puts one in mind of Dinesh D'Souza's observation about religious devotion. If complete submission is required from a faith tradition, then there is no such thing as piety. In other words, a faith tradition does which not allow deviation or debate cannot foster the unfettered expression of belief.

Only when freely given can any religious act be deemed holy. Coercion and fear is ungodly, no matter which deity is heading up the operation. The same goes for legislated coercion. It is not much consolation, but it will take an Act of Parliament to add Presumed Consent to the British legal statutes.

January 17, 2008

UK Political Observers View the Republican Dilemma

Sometimes a headline is worth 1000 words. Over a January 17 report out of South Carolina, the London Times nailed it. "The Republican Caravan Rolls on -- But Who Knows Where It's Going?" The article's author, Tom Baldwin, did not pull any punches. He characterized the Republican Party as being on a zigzag course, "fractured and disoriented."

The rest of the story was an apologetic tract in defense of John McCain. Baldwin talked about McCain's Truth Squad which was formed to prevent a recurrence of the negative attacks on the Senator in the run-up to the 2000 primary in the Palmetto State. Back then McCain was smeared with an unproven set of rumors that he (1) had fathered a child with a black woman and (2) had committed treason by collaborating with the enemy back in Vietnam. The Truth Squad was deployed to South Carolina to counter a fresh attempt to "swift boat" the Arizona Senator by a group called Vietnam Veterans Against John McCain.

Another Times commentator, Daniel Finkelstein, is betting on McCain to win the Republican Party's nomination after the equivalent of coming back from a political near death experience. Rudy is also on his short list, but McCain has momentum and Giuliani's star is fading. According to Finkelstein, Huckabee's best hope to get on the ticket is tied to Giuliani who might want to appease evangelicals by tapping the Arkansas preacher and former Governor as his VP. It must be said that secularist British reporters, sent to cover the campaign in the US, are hard put to write about the religious appeal of Huckabee. They have, however, duly noted that he has had to ground his press plane for lack of funds.

According to Tim Shipman, one of the Telegraph's US election observers, John McCain won South Carolina because he had the support of the Republican establishment, which will surely be news to them. Shipman gives the glory for McCain's SC win to his old pal, Fred Thompson, because Fred siphoned off a 20% share of conservative Christians which otherwise would have accrued to Mike Huckabee. Blog chatter has suggested that Fred could turn the candidacy tide by throwing his support behind McCain, a notion that horrifies those who saw Thompson as the only real conservative in the field.

But not all UK writers are happy about McCain landing on the top of the Republican ticket. The left leaning Independent's Johann Hart warned his readers not to be fooled by the myth of John McCain as a hero. Hart labels McCain as third generation "navy royalty, " raised like a prince by his father and grandfather. This monarchical messianic mindset, Hart asserts, makes McCain the candidate that the left should fear the most. Demonstrating a complete misreading of the facts, Hart say that McCain is an "uber hawk" who is "to the right of Bush on a whole range of subjects." Would that this were true. Sounds like another job for the Truth Squad.

Hart also reprises the details surrounding the Keating Five campaign contribution scandal, in which McCain was implicated, explaining that the Senator made a virtue of this career blot by becoming the champion of campaign finance reform. Again, the rejection of McCain-Feingold by the core of the conservative movement seems to have escaped Mr. Hart's attention, but who says that being right for all the wrong reasons isn't a good thing.

A comment posted to one of these articles brought up another past transgression which Senator McCain undoubtedly wishes had been lost in the mists of history. This involved an occasion when McCain was reprimanded and forced to apologize for saying that Chelsea Clinton was so ugly because her Father was actually Janet Reno. You can be sure this slight will be recalled at the most effective critical moment by Chelsea's Mother who will ask voters to contemplate McCain's skill as a diplomat on the world stage.

In a move that boggles the mind, the Conservative (Tory) Party leader, David Cameron has come out in favor of McCain. In a speech delivered at the international economic forum in Davos, Switzerland, Cameron singled out John McCain for taking a firm stand against protectionism. Specifically Cameron said: "In years to come, the world will look back at this period, and there will be heroes and there will be villains. The heroes will be those who held their nerve and stood up for free trade." Rosa Prince, a Daily Mirror journalist, jumped on Cameron's statement pointing out that overtly backing a candidate for the US Presidency broke with accepted diplomatic convention. But there is more. Writing for The Independent, Pandora -- by now, a clichéd nom de plume - asserted that junior (Tory) aides have already been told that a few of them will be heading across the Atlantic to work on the McCain campaign if he gets the nomination.

There are, of course, other odd observations embedded in the numerous British political articles and election blogs. One pundit believes that Mitt Romney will prevail because he can keep writing checks when the other candidates are running their campaigns on monetary fumes. On BritainandAmerica.com, Tim Montgomerie opines that the British media "could swing the next US election" because there is a growing US readership of London-sourced news, in particular (the left leaning) Guardian which provides "more feisty scrutiny of politicians."

And then there is this delicious fashion item posted on the UK Telegraph's "Trail Mix 2008" blog. It advises Barack Obama to put on a tie, especially when he wears white shirts, because going without one makes him look "forgetful."

January 28, 2008

Archbishop of Canterbury Gone Bonkers

When even the religion reporter for the Times of London has to ask if the Archbishop of Canterbury has gone bonkers, the question has become rhetorical. The answer is all too obvious.

Last Thursday morning, February 7, Rowan Williams -- the Archbishop of Canterbury, top man in the hierarchy of the Church of England -- took to the airwaves. In a BBC Radio Four interview, he said that the United Kingdom will eventually have to adopt Islamic Sharia Law -- on a limited basis -- on the premise that this will create social cohesion.

His words have had quite an impact -- perhaps best compared to the effect of dropping a suitcase nuke into the room at high tea in Buckingham Palace. If there were any English still sleep walking through the destruction of their national identity, the ultimate wake up call just came.

When Henry the 8th wanted a divorce and the Catholic Pope would not give it to him, the Church of England was born. Henry not only broke the bonds of fealty to the Pope, he seized all the property held by the Roman Church, dissolved their monasteries, killed or banished the Catholic clergy, and forced all surviving remnants of Catholicism in England underground for centuries.

While he was at it, Henry ended all foreign ecclesiastical jurisdiction over his Kingdom and made all future monarchs the titular head of the Anglican Church. Henry's daughter, Queen Elizabeth the First, fleshed out this policy. She decreed that the break with Rome restored to the Crown, "the ancient jurisdiction over the state -- ecclesiastical and spiritual -- abolishing all foreign power repugnant to the same." This is not just an opinion. It is an Article in the founding document of the Church of England.

The Times' religion editor, Ruth Gledhill, reviews this history and then adds her own ironic observation. "And now Queen Elizabeth II's very own Archbishop -- and let's not forget she is his Church's Supreme Governor - wants to introduce a new jurisdiction into this realm of England. And an Islamic one at that!"

For those who might not be up to speed on Sharia law, it is not like The Ten Commandments or the Bill of Rights. It is not just Holy Law; it is wholly Holy secular law too. It is the all-inclusive law as imposed by a theocratic state. It governs everything from banking to marriage. And it carries some pretty heavy penalties, from cutting off the hands of thieves to stoning women caught in adultery, even if the adultery stems from a gang rape. It also looks the other way when fathers, brothers, or uncles kill family females who dare to date outside of Islam. These are known as "honor killings."

The Archbishop of Canterbury supports his partially pro-Sharia law position by citing the inherent inequity which ensues when Catholic adoption agencies discriminate against gay couples. Of course, there are no gay people in Iran according to Ahmadinejad so that isn't the best illustration the Archbishop might have chosen to make his point. In fact, instances of sharia law being carried out within British Muslim communities have been reported. A young man who knifed someone was judged by a Sharia court and let out on the streets when his family compensated his victim financially.

You might wonder what the current Prime Minister of the United Kingdom has said in reaction to this statement by the head of the Anglican Church. Surprise! He hedged his bets. Gordon Brown was already on record as saying that there are small areas in which concessions to Sharia Law could be made, but also stipulated that Sharia Law could not be used as a justification for breaching English law. To this apparent contradiction a spokesperson added: "The Prime Minister believes British law should apply in this country, based on British values." Right. Clear on that are we?

The Archbishop has elaborated on Gordon Brown's stance

by stating: "it is a misunderstanding to suppose that people don't have other affiliations, other loyalties which shape and dictate how they behave in society and the law needs to take some account of that." And in another quote, the Archbishop claims: "...there are ways of looking at marital disputes, for example, which provide an alternative to the divorce courts as we understand them."

This led one person in the Telegraph's comment section to ask if attendees to Sharia stonings in the UK would have to buy tickets or would they be open to the public? The furore (British spelling) had reached such a fever pitch that on Friday the BBC World Service devoted its one-hour call-in program -- "Have Your Say" -- to this topic. (The program can be downloaded from the BBC.co.uk website). Calls came in from around the world and perhaps the most compelling was from a man in Saudi Arabia who wanted to know when the Archbishop would be visiting that nation, one in which Christian churches are not allowed. Over and over again, people keep asking the bleeding obvious question. "When is the Archbishop of Canterbury going to stand up and represent the Christian faith?

This is not the first time that Rowan Williams has done something which suggests he is bonkers. Before he was "enthroned" as the ABC, Williams had himself inducted into the Druids, an ancient pagan faith group. More recently, he argued for the abolition of the blasphemy law - as long as it was replaced by something even more severe. People should be punished for daring to voice thoughts that were hurtful to others, he said, even when that hurt was unintentional."

This sounds like a description of the nanny state dressed as a dominatrix. And yes, one is aware that a line has been crossed when the Archbishop of Canterbury and Britney Spears appear to be exhibiting the same self destructive and delusional bipolar behaviors. If he is hearing all the voices, Williams cannot have missed those who are calling out: "Off with his head." By Saturday, photos of the man with a pair of the wildest eyebrows in Christendom were splashed across the front pages of British broadsheets and tabloids. The Archbishop of Canterbury seemed genuinely incapable of understanding the calls for his resignation. Even the second most powerful cleric in England, the Archbishop of York, a native of Africa, Dr. John Sentamu, has said sharia law in England would never happen. The best Rowan Williams got by way of support came from The Muslim Council of Britain and all they did was to characterize his ideas as "thoughtful." Damned with faint praise if you ask me. And rightly so.

Treason? Certainly. But in these mad days, to paraphrase the aphorism, treason prospers so none dare call it treason.

February 11, 2008

Putin Foe Dead in the UK

It is suggestive that this story was filed by in the UK Telegraph by a chap identified as the "Security Correspondent."

Here are the initial facts behind the headline. An exiled billionaire from the sovereign Republic of Georgia -- as in the former Soviet Union not the US state -- was discovered with his post-Soviet toes turned up in the glorious London suburb of Surrey. It is clear that he did not pass away from the ravages of old age. Akkadi "Badri" Patarkatsishvili -- the wealthiest man from his part of the old empire -- was a seasoned 52 when he died. Friends (who might be a tad nervous) ascribe his demise to heart failure. His obits characterize him as a "charismatic oligarch." You have to love the lingo.

"Badri" moved to England after he reportedly received repeated threats on his life.

A rich man has his life threatened? Who wrote this copy -- Agatha Christie?

It is natural to draw a squiggley -- not straight -- line back to the death of Alexander Litvienko, whose death has already left a deep rift in UK- ex USSR relations. As reported in this same space, Litvinenko wrote his own tell-all about the misdeeds of the Putin people and was dispatched for his trouble. The method by which Litvinenko met his maker had a rather quirky cultural twist. The former KGB agent (and let's not forget Putin is a member of that club too) succumbed to the side effects of fallout from sipping a cuppa Polonium-laced radioactive tea.

Now we come to the demise of Mr. Patarkatsishvili who refused to return to Georgia claiming his life was in danger and that at least two previous attempts to kill him, in Britain, had failed. The reason he had been targeted was -- ostensibly -- that he wanted to run for the office of the President of the Republic of Georgia. For this run, Badri claimed, one's reputation had to be "crystal clear." What was his platform? Who felt threatened enough to kill him?

Let us recall that Eduard Shevardnadze was the first elected President of the Republic of Georgia when the old Soviet Union disassembled itself with a little help from the Gipper.

He was on the scene back in 1986 when, with Gorbachev, the terms of the end of the Cold War evolved. He helped delineate and encouraged the idea that the former USSR's eastern European satellites could "do it their way" (known as the Sinatra Doctrine) as opposed to being forced to adopt a uniform policy or enforced model of democratization. Great tribulation ensued and that leads one to wonder about who would have it in for Mr. Patarkatsishvili? What philosophy did he represent which might be a threat to anyone in the days of President Putin's new Russia? Who on the political scene would want to see him eliminated? There are plenty of suspects a la Ms. Christie, and no lack of plotters.

Badri felt he had to stay in England to save his life. Putin's people claim that they had nothing to do with Badri's early departure. And Badri's spokespeople say that they had no knowledge of secret tapes in which Badri allegedly offer to pay for the assassination of a government minister back in Georgia.

The now late billionaire had been in the bidding process to acquire the West Ham United football (i.e., soccer) club, and once reputedly told the press: "The way they are going is proving they have only one plan -- to get rid of me." So Badri dropped out of the Georgian Presidential race because of "black PR," (lovely new term) which was linked to his desire to acquire a football team. Football is, for all intents and purposes, the religion of England. Sectarian violence can break out between team supporters who have too many pints of beers or just don't like the outcome of any given game. Hooliganiam has become as strong an "ISM" as any ever witnessed in the British Isles and the same goes for the rest of a football mad world. The NFL pales in comparison.

So here we are in America, fussing over the separation of church and state and what we obviously ought to be concerned about is the separation of state and football. Can you see the day when we elect a President on the same day as the Superbowl? What will the networks charge for those ads? Blimey. The mind boggles and -- by the way -- who dunnit?

February 14, 2008

Forced Marriages and Unforeseen Consequences

Earlier this month, the UK Independent newspaper ran the following headline: "A question of honor: Police say 17,000 women are victims every year." An "honor victim" is any woman whose liberty and wellbeing is threatened, or whose life is ended, as the outcome of a forced marriage somehow gone awry. A forced marriage is defined as one that is contracted, without consent of either the bride or the groom, for the purpose of gaining economic or social advantage, especially the right of residency in the spouse's country.

In the past decade or so, the rise of Muslim and other immigrant communities within the United Kingdom has brought the cultural tradition of the forced marriage to this already troubled island. Such marriages are illegal contracts according to the laws of the United Kingdom, as well as violations of basic human rights as defined by the Untied Nations. Muslims deny that Islam promotes such arranged relationships, though there is much evidence to the contrary. But the arranged marriage is standard practice among Asian communities. To be very clear, "Asian" is the term the British use as a designation for people whose countries of origin are primarily Bangladesh, India, and Pakistan.

With that understood, let's unpack the headline figure.

There are four subcategories of honor victims. The first of these are the psychological victims who are unable to defy the pressure to enter a forced marriage. According to a recent report published by The Centre for Social Cohesion, many such women (exact toll unknown) suffer anxiety, deep depressions, and other psychological problems. Their anguish at not being able to comply with family expectations often leads them to self-harm, schizophrenia, and suicide.

Some honor victims are listed as assault cases. The families of these victims take brutal exception when a daughter -- or son -- rebels against a forced marriage or appears to be succumbing to the corrupt values of western culture. Dating -- or worse falling in love with someone outside the family religion -- is also unacceptable. Daughters who rebel against a forced marriage can be beaten within an inch of their lives, disfigured, or disabled.

Young Muslim women in western dress who turn up bloodied in emergency wards are easily spotted, but significant cuts and bruises can be hidden beneath head-to-toe Muslim garb. Escape is often impossible, especially if a young woman's family locks her up at home until she submits. If she suffers scars and disfigurement, she will not be inclined to attempt re-entry into western society. Should the young woman have a personal checking or savings account, community bankers have been known to oblige a family's request for a complete withdrawal, no questions asked.

Some honor victims are counted as "missing." These are the ones who vanish without a trace. Take for example the town of Bradford. Located up north in Yorkshire, halfway between England's east and west coasts, Bradford's population is a relatively modest 240,000. Last year, 250 -- yes -- two hundred and fifty -- girls between the ages of 13 and 16 left their classrooms in Bradford and never returned to school. When questioned by the authorities, these families explained that their teenage daughters had failed to return from trips abroad. If this sort of mass trafficking occurs within a single little town, small wonder the UK Police assert the national total of honor victims has reached the rate of 17,000 per year.

Finally -- quite finally -- we come to the category known as honor killings. These victims are, perhaps, the bravest of young women. They refuse to give up their western ways, date outside their tradition, and will not submit to a forced marriage. Their murders are usually carried out by an irate father, or by an assortment of brothers, uncles, or male cousins. Attempts to disguise their deaths as suicides or accidents are not always a success. Inconvenient corpses have been found buried in back gardens, tossed into the nearest river, or burned in metal trash bins.

Of those 17,000 headlined honor victim cases in 2007, the UK Police assert that only about one dozen were honor killings. Only. That's a far cry from India (which is predominantly Hindu) where about 5000 brides are annually figured to be victims of honor killings, usually because their marriage dowries were deemed insufficient. It's a matter of percentages and cultural relativity.

In 2003 the Metropolitan Police formed a task force to investigate forced marriages. A specialist unit was assigned to research cases of possible honor crimes -- and also to review 100 suspicious murder files going back over the previous decade.

This effort has since inspired the British government to create The Forced Marriage Unit -- a department fused between the UK Home and Foreign Offices. The FMU claims that last year it received 5000 requests to investigate possible instances of forced marriages. It was able to pursue only 400 of the cases brought to its attention. Of that number, FMU Interventions resulted in the rescue and return of 167 Britons who had been sent out by their families to enter into forced marriages. For the record, this is not just a women's issue. Fifteen percent of FMU cases involve young men and boys who, like their female counterparts, can be honor victims.

But as the FMU numbers reveal, the vast majority of Britons sent abroad to enter into forced marriages are not found and repatriated. They marry and bring their spouses back into Britain according to the family plan. Their spouses are frequently first cousins, but this is far more than a Passport Ponzi Scheme. It is more than a human rights issue. It is a cultural practice that is bringing forth a tragic set of unforeseen consequences for the victims.

When first cousins marry, their offspring are inclined to have birth defects far above the national average. The National Health Service has just released its first accounting of the number of children -- the products of forced marriages between cousins -- who suffer from birth defects. The statistics are staggering. For example, one in three of all babies born to British Pakistanis -- who account for 3 percent of all UK births -- have genetic illnesses. In that town of Bradford, in a school where 90 percent of the students are Pakistani and Bangladeshi children, cases of autism and an array of learning and physical disabilities, are the rule not the exception. When the authorities try to intervene on behalf of the children, they generally discover the mothers speak no English. They are the forced brides who have been imported from "back home."

There are a growing number of non-governmental organizations, including The Muslim Parliament of Great Britain (a story in itself) which are active in trying to end forced marriages. Multiculturalists insist that the problem is not a product of religion, but of tradition. Those who are critical of the practice are, predictably, labeled as racists. Two haunting questions confront the British: How many more women have to die before the society wakes up? How many more children will be impaired for life before forced marriages end?

February 25, 2008

David Cameron Takes on Multi-Culturalism

On February 26, a UK think-tank -- The National and International Security Group -- released its interim report on social cohesion. The findings inspired Conservative Party leader David Cameron to give his strongest speech ever on the pitfalls and failures generated by multiculturalism. The next morning at 12:54 am, a 5.3 earthquake shook England awake. It was the largest temblor to hit Britain in a decade. Mere coincidence?

The Security Group stated outright what many Britons and Americans had concluded long ago: that unrestrained multiculturalism had resulted in attitudes that encouraged differences at the expense of the greater social whole. By stressing such differences, the report asserted, Muslim organizations in the UK had been able to use multicultural ideology to give greater weight to their own views.

The report found: "As Muslim communities enter the third generation of settlement in this country, and in circumstances where a rapidly rising proportion have been educated here, it is anomalous and patronising to individuals to treat them indirectly as members of a group and not directly as citizens in their own individual right on a par with other voters."

Mr. Cameron went a little farther when he accused some Muslim associations of deliberately using multiculturalism to promote an "us versus them" paradigm. These organizations had created their political power bases by fostering "ghettoization."

Self-imposed segregation was credited with creating a generation of young Muslims who feel like aliens in their own country. For their sense of identity, they have turned toward Islamic radicalism, both within small local cells or as members of larger extremist movements. While he was at it, Cameron took aim at the Archbishop of Canterbury's recent suggestion that a smidgeon of Sharia Law could be tacked on to work in tandem with the British legal system. The Tory leader said that the application of this "dangerous and illiberal" idea would result in "legal apartheid" and could further undermine Britain's already shaky sense of collective national identity. Experts in the bleeding obvious, these think tank folks, but clearly they assisted Mr. Cameron, in lifting the veil at last.

By week's end, the newspapers were full of photos of fallen chimneys and assorted scattered bits of masonry. Tales of near misses were giving some folks their 15 minutes of fame. Amid this post-quake coverage, two other major stories emerged to shake up the British public.

The first was neatly compacted into this headline: "Bobbies will be taught sharia law and the Koran in a secret plan to counter terror at the local level." The explanation given for turning police stations into mini-madrassas (Islamic religious schools) was not just to provide multicultural sensitivity training, but to help the coppers ferret out budding extremists. Critics suggested that this kind of training would, in fact, turn crime fighters into defacto religious police squads, trained like sniffer dogs to pick up the scent of Islamic radicals, just as the religious fashion police in Iran go looking for girls whose hijabs aren't up to snuff.

One Conservative MP groaned: "Police officers are not there to implement sharia law. They are there to implement British law. We will only get community cohesion when everybody signs up to being British and following British law." Police authorities insisted that this theological training for bobbies was "part of a wide-ranging strategy to prevent extremist ideas gaining hold in primary schools, colleges, the internet, and prisons." For example, to help nip things in the bud, the police would henceforth be expected to give guidance to parents on how to stop their offspring from searching out extremist websites. This practice would presumably be carried out on a door-to-door basis or with the help of psychics.

For a touch of complete irony, this "Prevent Plan" (as it has been tagged) was formulated after yet another piece of research discovered that because Muslims did not trust the police, they were unlikely to call in tips about extremist activities in their communities. Somehow this revelation was translated into the vision of teaching the Koran to the cops as a trust-building exercise. As the Archbishop of Canterbury has said, the UK has to "face up to the fact" that some of its citizens do not relate to the British legal system and therefore Muslims should not have to choose between "the stark alternatives of cultural loyalty or state loyalty."

Is your head spinning yet?

The other big secret let out of the bag was that Prince Harry had been serving in Afghanistan since Christmas. Matt Drudge was identified as the culprit in fingering Harry's undercover soldiering. It seems that the British press corps, both print and broadcast, had taken a solemn oath to keep Harry's secret, which they did. This has since given rise to a raging debate on how much the press can be trusted if they can keep such a big secret from the public. The discussion amusingly presumes such trust was a pre-existing condition.

Harry was quickly whisked back to England where he was greeted by some as a hero who had done the British proud. In return, Harry gave an interview in which he said Army food was rubbish, he didn't get his Father's Christmas card until February, and if he couldn't be a regular soldier he was going off to live in Africa because -- truth to tell -- he doesn't like England all that much. So there.

Reactions to Harry's deployment from Islamic quarters were pretty predictable. They claimed that by shooting at the resurgent Taliban he had made the Royal family legitimate targets for retribution. It was now a personal thing. One hopes that the fellows who guard Buckingham Palace are not thumbing through the Koran when retaliatory attacks are attempted by bands of angry multiculturalists.

March 4, 2008

Turkey Risks Reforming Islam's Holy Texts

Turkey has been on the EU's "Candidate Country List" since 1999. The principal obstacle -- aside from the pseudo-war between Greece and Turkey over the island nation of Cyprus -- is how Turkey tries to balance religion and politics.

It is a one-off hybrid. Doubts persist over its ability to remain a modern secular, yet Islamic, state. Fears that Europe is evolving into Eurabia run high. Those against Turkey's accession sometimes invoke the old line about what happens once the camel gets his nose under your tent flap.

British Prime Minister Gordon Brown has decided to uphold Tony Blair's commitment to champion Turkey's bid for EU membership. But early last month, German Chancellor Angela Merkel and French President Nicholas Sarkozy jointly renewed their opposition to having Turkey become the 28th fully accepted EU member nation. The best they were willing to offer was privileged partnership status, pending Turkey's ability to conform to a slew of non-negotiable EU membership requirements. A number of these involve agreeing to accept EU policies on human rights. One mildly amusing demand is that Turkey eliminate Article 301 from its Penal Code. That would be the law which forbids "insulting Turkishness." Those found guilty of committing a 301 are looking at a four-year jail term.

The Turks are very sensitive when it comes to national pride, including the Islamic nexus of its cultural identity, which is why the latest theological news out of Turkey caught lots of folks by surprise.

Turkey is attempting what may be nothing less than an Islamic Reformation. The Turkish Martin Luthers -- at enormous risk to themselves and their government -- are trying to reinterpret the basic law of Islam.

The significance of that cannot be understated: the radical Islamic nations -- Iran, Saudi Arabia and all the others -- regard the Koran and the hadiths (the sayings of Mohammed that are the basis for the only permissible interpretations of the Koran -- are perfect and not subject to interpretation, as Westerners interpret Christianity and Judaism.

Two weeks ago the Turkish government's powerful Department of Religious Affairs (the Diyanet) announced that 35 religious scholars, in the Theology Department at Ankara University, were nearly finished a three-year forensic examination of the Islamic Hadiths. After the Qu'ran (Koran), the Hadiths are the second most sacred text in Islam. They are the sayings and deeds of Mohammed and constitute a handbook on how to live as a devout Muslim. Ninety percent of Sharia Law is based on the Hadiths.

There have not been any attempts to open the text to new interpretations since 1400. In that year, the reigning Caliphate (based in Turkey) proclaimed that Islam had reached such a state of perfection that no further modifications to the Hadiths were necessary. However quietly, some Islamic scholars question the authenticity of some of the sayings since they were handed down through oral traditions. Others are seen as anachronisms. The scholars cite prohibitions about women traveling alone as an example of what can be revised. In the days of Mohammed, traveling was a dangerous proposition. The old laws do not have the same context in modern society, although attempts to alter the overall status of women continue to generate friction. The wearing of headscarves (hijabs) is a hotly debated issue. On the other hand, Turkey has made strides in ending forced marriages and comes down hard on those who carry out honor killings against unwilling (usually very young) brides.

For Turkey's government to "bless" this reinterpretation of passages in the Hadith came as a shock to many Muslims. To an unknown number of Wahabbi terrorists, it is down right heretical. Turkey knew that the announcement could have evoked violent reactions. That none have occurred -- so far -- is significant.

When the BBC broke this news, observers in the West were

similarly stunned. Was this a sign of a coming détente in the clash of civilizations? Was Islam ready to initiate its own Reformation? Cynics wondered if Turkey wanted EU membership so badly that it was willing to risk an Islamic backlash just to further its chances. Was this just a stunt?

In fairness, the Turkish government, elected last July, has done much to innovate both its domestic and international policies. Its recent eight-day incursion into Iraq to squash Kurdish rebels raised eyebrows, but the EU and USA did supply intell to the Turkish military in support of the objective. Once the troops were back across the border, Turkey immediately announced plans to invest $12 billion in the impoverished - predominantly Kurdish -- southeast corner of the country. There are 12 million Kurds living in Turkey -- one sixth of the entire population. The idea is to win the hearts and minds of the Kurds and turn them against the independence-seeking rebels. Turkey's Prime Minister, Tayyip Erdogan, described the investment package as fighting terrorism on psychological and socio-economic levels. This plan includes creating a Kurdish language television channel, building two dams, creating a network of water canals, paving roads, and removing landmines along the Syrian border.

The blogosphere has, predictably, erupted with conflicting points of view on the Hadith reformation. The naysayers condemn Islam as nothing but "imperialism with a religious face." A chorus of voices warned that this religious refinement is all smoke and mirrors and that Islam cannot change without recanting the violent edicts in the Qu'ran. The optimists are guarded. The general consensus from that quarter is that updating the Hadiths will do nothing to end jihadist movements, but Turkey's endeavor to open the doors of theological inquiry should be applauded. The EU has made no statement regarding the Hadith revisions. Methinks the jury remains hung.

But Turkey's actions will reverberate far beyond the EU. They are -- in the ideological war in which we are engaged – much more important than what France thinks of Turks' culture.

March 17, 2008

Osama and the Pope

In early March, the media had a field day announcing that Pope Benedict XVI had issued a list of "new sins." As with many reports on religion, the new sins articles were slathered with self-satisfied secular glee. They were also wrong. The story started spinning when comments -- made to a group of priests by a Cardinal on the subject of hearing confessions -- were made public. The Cardinal's goal was to underscore that moral choices were not limited to what we did when alone, but also included what we do as citizens of the world. Hence, the Cardinal's focus on caring for the environment, preventing pollution, and ending poverty, as acts of social responsibility. The Pope was asked to comment on the Cardinal's remarks when he met with the group later, but there was no list. The Pope didn't try to upstage Moses or Jesus.

Thankfully the spin cycle was abbreviated by Wednesday of Holy Week, (March 18th), when the attention of the media was transfixed by the latest pronouncement from the elusive Al Qaeda mastermind. His words inspired Matt Drudge to run an all caps red-letter headline: "Bin Laden Slams Pope." Certain members of the press sustained a serious case of whiplash. More than one must have (secretly) wondered how that purported list of new sins could have caused bin Laden go ballistic at Benedict. Then came the transcript of the tape in which bin Laden attributed his wrath to the planned reprinting of a dozen controversial Danish cartoons, first published two years ago, that satirize Islam and the Prophet Mohammed. This time around, Bin Laden was not focusing his threats solely at the Danes. This time he told the entire EU to beware. And -- just in time for Easter -- Osama shared his latest pet conspiracy theory. He asserted that the decision to reprint the cartoons was part of a nefarious Papal plot designed to gin up a new Christian Crusade against the Muslim world. Nice cover story, but there are several other provocations afoot -- any one of which could have put the wind up the terrorist kingpin.

Back on March 5th, Vatican officials and a visiting group of five Muslim leaders agreed to establish a permanent dialogue. The first meeting of The Catholic Muslim Forum is scheduled for early November of 2008 in Rome. The Pope will deliver a message to the 24 attendees. This announcement comes two years after remarks Benedict made -- at his former university home, in Regensburg, Germany -- which angered many Muslims. A passage in the Pope's speech was interpreted as an accusation that that Islam was violent and irrational.

The misunderstanding, for which the Pope expressed regret, resulted in the deaths of about 50 people and a bit of property destruction by indignant Islamists. It also prompted 138 Muslim scholars to pen and sign "Common Word," an appeal for the Vatican and other Christian church leaders to enter into a dialogue because "the very survival of the world itself" depended on it. Since the document was created, the number of Muslim signatories has grown to 240. As Ibrahim Kalin, of Turkey's Seta Foundation, noted: "Muslims and Christians make up about 55 percent of the world and there will be no peace in the world unless there is peace between the two communities." Of course, the crucial question for many will be: Peace at What Cost?

Osama is -- no doubt -- also reeling from fresh territorial issues. Only days before his Crusade tirade, the first (ever) Catholic Church opened its doors in Doha, Qatar. Services at Our Lady of the Rosary will be held in 14 languages to accommodate the estimated 150,000 -- predominantly Catholic Christians -- from 100 countries, who reside in Qatar. The first worship service -- attended by thousands of people -- was held under heavy security, but it went off without disruption. The mass was led by the Pope's special envoy, the Prefect of the Congregation for the Evangelization of Peoples, (a red flag title if there ever was one to devout Muslims) Cardinal Ivan Dias. Vatican Radio described this event as one "of historical importance which, after 14 centuries of prohibitions, sees a place of worship for Catholics established." Mind you, the building in which worshippers gather has no outward symbols of Christianity -- no crosses or bells -- but the land on which the structure stands was donated by Qatar's Emir (Sheikh Hamad Bin

Khalifa Al-Thani) - in power since a coup in 1995. The Emir favors interreligious dialogue. Not so all of his ministers, one of whom has asked for a countrywide referendum before other Christian churches are approved.

That same week, news began to circulate that the Vatican was negotiating to open a Catholic Church in Saudi Arabia. This possibility emerged following King Abdullah's visit to the Vatican last November, where he was welcomed by the Pope. The man in charge of this dialogue is Archbishop Mounged El-Hachem, the papal envoy to Kuwait, Qatar, Bahrain, Yemen and the United Arab Emirates. That title speaks volumes. Although all Saudi citizens are required by law to be Muslims, opening a Catholic church in Saudi is viewed -- by both parties -- as a sign that reciprocity and respect between Islam and Christianity is not impossible.

Now if 9-11 was a protest against the US military presence in the Middle East, most specifically Saudi Arabia, just imagine how annoyed Bin Laden must be about King Abdullah giving permission for Christian churches to be established on Muslim turf. But wait -- there's more.

The Saudi Arabian government has just announced that 40,000 Imams will be "retrained" to eliminate extremist tendencies in their teachings. (Maybe they can reserve a space for Rev. Wright). According to Al-Sharq al Awsat, a prominent Saudi newspaper, five years ago, a Saudi Ministry of Religious Affairs and Center for Religious Dialogue was inaugurated to disseminate a more moderate interpretation of Islamic tradition and encourage religious tolerance. Imam retraining is part of the plan. Since the Center was created, at least 1000 Imams -- judged to be inciting youth to join the global jihad -- have been banished from their mosques. When King Abdullah visited the Bush Ranch in Texas, there were snickers about oil and family deals. But it turns out that the President was negotiating with the Saudi King to "rein in" militant clerics. Some observers are quick to point out that this may only be an exercise in superficial shuffling for the sake of appearances. Time will tell.

Another straw -- piled on to help break the camel's back -- came during the Easter Vigil this past weekend when the Pope officiated at the baptism of seven people. Among that select group was the Egyptian (and Muslim) born Magdi Allam -- now a Catholic convert -- who serves as Deputy Editor of Italy's Corriere delia Sera paper and is a noted commentator on Muslim and Arab Affairs.

Small wonder Osama is succumbing to dark conspiratorial thoughts. He must be terrified to ask himself "what next?" Can't you just picture him -- in a state of religious frenzy -- desperately trying to find some Alka Seltzer or a couple of aspirins in his militant Islamic medicine chest?

March 24, 2008

Gordon Frankenbrown's Brave New Labor

March came in like a mad hatter in England. This included a White Easter which dusted the countryside with picturesque snow. Less attractive was the eruption of a heated debate among politicians, scientists, and the clergy. With his usual lack of timing, Prime Minister Gordon Brown chose the earliest pre-Easter season in decades to re-introduce a bill through which the government would bless the creation of hybrid embryos.

Hybrid embryos aren't designed to give better mileage out of a bowl of porridge. Scientists involved in stem cell research would be allowed to create interspecies entities made from injecting human DNA into hollowed out animal egg cells. The end product would be 99.9 percent human and 0.1 percent animal. The technology is the same one that produced Dolly, the world's famous first cloned sheep.

News of the proposed Human Fertilization and Embryology Bill was met with unusually boisterous opposition from leading Catholic prelates and caused some of the Labour Party's own Catholic members to threaten an insurgency. Reporters had a field day writing headlines invoking Frankenstein. From his pulpit on Easter Sunday, Cardinal Keith O'Brien, head of the Catholic Church in Brown's native Scotland, called for the bill to be rejected as it represented "a monstrous attack on human rights, human dignity, and human life." This sentiment was echoed in many other sermons, preached to the full houses which tend to gather on the most holy day in the Christian calendar.

As one might expect, the scientific community of Britain responded with explanations on how religious people had gotten it all wrong, again. Stem cell biologists and experts in human genetics gave media interviews full of relativistic arguments (everyone else is already doing this) and sang the club theme song about the untold numbers of people who would be miraculously healed using stem cells (almost like raising folks from the dead wholesale). The Bill also provides for the creation of "saviour siblings." This term refers to creating a batch of family embryos in order to find a match for an existing child with a specific disease. The "saviour" is carried to term, at which point its placenta, bone marrow, or what have you is harvested and he or she gets to live. Meanwhile, the other embryos could be legally destroyed, tossed in the bin presumably marked: Disposable Replacement Spare Parts.

Another highly controversial section of the Bill would permit the biological father of a child conceived -- via in-vitro fertilization -- to be removed from a birth certificate and replaced with the name of another unrelated parent. The joint select committee of MP's assigned to review this legislation moaned that this amounted to, "the state colluding in a deception." Yes, the same Brave New World Labour Party that has run the National Health Service into the ground now offers to wipe the biological slate clean, for they argue that a sperm donor ought not to be responsible for any child he fathers. This puts children one small step away from having the government claim paternity from the get-go.

The Cardinal's position was that scientists failed to comprehend the theological stance against playing God. He also renewed his call for Gordon Brown to allow Catholic members of Labour who opposed the Bill to vote their consciences without the threat of being sacked (fired) for their faith.

Enter the infamous "floated compromise" maneuver.

Faced with the Easter onslaught, the media received word -- from the Brown shop -- that Members of Parliament who were deeply concerned about the Bill might be granted permission to hold their seats by voting against just the parts they didn't like. Everyone else would then vote for the whole Bill and it would pass. When one of the rebellious MP's labeled this "beyond cynical," the most senior member of the Catholic clergy entered the crossfire.

Cardinal Cormac Murphy O'Connor, leader of the Roman Church in England and Wales, went public to insist that Labour

MP's should be granted what is known as a "free vote," the process by which party members are allowed to vote their minds as opposed to being required to succumb to party pressure to vote as an ideological block. O'Connor also encouraged Catholic Cabinet Ministers in Brown's government, as well as any from other faiths, to stand up and be counted in this matter. By March 23, up to a dozen Labour rebels were talking about turning in their resignations. A document known as "the doomsday list" began to circulate.

Brown sustained a further blow when -- at mid-week -- Steven Byers, the respected former Trade and Industry Cabinet Secretary, and a non Catholic, spoke out loudly in a bid to reach Brown's tin political ear. This was considered a direct challenge to the Prime Minster's authority.

And lest you wonder where the Conservative leadership was in this affair, David Cameron pointed out that his MP's have been granted permission for a "free vote" and challenged Brown to do likewise. Should he fail to do so, Cameron predicted that Brown would be forced to "climb down" from his inflexible position and endure another public humiliation. But the Tory Party leader stopped far short of calling for a cease and desist on all stem cell and embryonic research. It is a curious footnote to this situation (which is unlikely to be resolved until May) that Gordon Brown and David Cameron each have a son with genetic diseases, either or both of whom might benefit from successful stem cell therapies.

*Post-script: As we went to press on Tuesday night, British newspapers carried the news that a team -- based at Newcastle upon Tyne University -- had created an embryo formed from injecting human skin cells into the hollowed-out egg cells of a cow. Despite protests that this was not a Frankenstein moment, The Daily Mail article reported that the egg was successfully "jolted" into life. The embryo survived for three days. The article goes on to say: "The scientists were only given permission to carry out the controversial experiment in January and the speed of their success has astonished scientists."

This leads one to wonder why there is going to be a vote -- one month from now -- on making hybrid experiments legal in the UK. Who gave this team permission to go ahead in January?

*Another postscript to this story: Gordon Brown did, indeed, "climb down" and gave his party members the right to a "free vote" on the Embryology Bill.

April 2, 2008

London Heathrow's New Terminal Five

The first passengers to arrive at London Heathrow's brand new Terminal Five last week had great travel expectations, but many never reached their destinations. Their flights were delayed, if not cancelled. However, some of their suitcases went on unexpected trips…like to Scotland and Italy…. by FedEx.

In British English, what happened at Terminal Five is called a "cock-up." It is a term generally used (even in polite society) to refer to things done badly by politicians. For once, the pols were not the immediate or sole cause of this particular "cock-up." The history of Terminal Five is somewhat tortured. Here are the gory details about how globalization may have inadvertently sunk another vessel of the British Empire.

In 1993, the British Airport Authority (BAA) submitted a planning application for what is now Terminal Five. In order to receive permission to build anything, UK government rules require parties to hold public hearings so that everyone can have their say. In this case, did they ever. For a start, no less than 700 conditions impacted the plan. One hundred hectares of the site (about the size of Hyde Park) had to be excavated by a team of 80 archaeologists. This amounted to the UK's largest ever single-site archaeological excavation. They dug stuff up from 8,500 years ago. Residents decried noise pollution. Green Protesters broke through Heathrow's perimeter and mounted sit-ins on building cranes.

Finally, on November 20, 2001, after 3.8 years (46 months) of hearings and debates (the longest discourse of its kind in British history), the construction of Terminal five (T5) was finally approved. Before a spade of earth was turned, Terminal Five had cost its proponents, BAA and BA, £63 million. Now here's the part where we really go global.

In 2006, BAA (now BAA Ltd) was taken over by a consortium, Grupo Ferrovial, which is based in Spain. GF owns 65% of Naples International Airport in Italy, and seven airports in the UK (Heathrow, Gatwick, Stansted, Glasgow, Edinburgh, Aberdeen and Southampton). BAA Limited also has international and subsidiary operations in Boston's Logan, Baltimore Washington (aka Thurgood Marshall Airport), and Indianapolis International.

Last week, five years and £4.3 billion ($8.6 billion) later, Terminal Five opened to the public with great fanfare. British Airways (currently the sole occupant of T5 – Virgin Atlantic declined a slot) boasted that the facility could handle 30 million travelers a year. This was over and above the 90 million who already transit in and out of Heathrow annually. T5 had all the modern conveniences and was upscale to the max. McDonalds was to be banished in favor of a Gordon Ramsey gourmet restaurant. Sixty-five escalators -- including the second longest in all of England -- would move those millions up and down with ease. Ninety-six "fast bag drop desks" (a post 9-11 pause for thought) promised a unique flow through system for passenger check-ins. Eleven miles of high tech systems and "track" were laid in order to handle up to 5000 bags an hour. And that's where it all seems to have gone wrong.

A software glitch in the computerized baggage handling system ultimately separated between 15,000 to 28,000 people (estimates vary) from their worldly travel goods. Within a day, Terminal Five became known as a place where baggage (and holiday dreams) went to die. Comparisons to another British engineering failure, the Titanic, were not infrequent. But was this really a British failure?

Grupo Ferrovial had subcontracted out virtually all T-5 systems and services to a bevy of international corporations. The Specifications List (of suspects) is available online.

Thinking that any new operation could have a bad first day, T5 remained open for business over this past weekend, but its appetite for baggage went unsatisfied.

Supermodel Naomi Campbell (known for her anger management issues) provided comic relief when -- upon learning one of her designer bags was missing -- spit on a policeman who eventually long hauled her designer body off a BA plane.

Alas, by then, so many suitcases had landed among the tombs of the unknown luggage, that the reuniting effort became impossible to achieve in-house. At this juncture, someone in a position of authority decided to out source the problem. And why by truck? Because the new rules say that you can't have luggage on a plane if the owner is not identified.

Bags from some UK flights were diverted to Stansted Airport. Others went by large vans to Manchester and Scotland because British Airways (BA) felt that that bags which belonged to European mainland customers needed to be sorted in a special facility. This explains how an untold number of suitcases were trucked to Milan, Italy. Adding insult to injury, one British pundit quipped that the Italian option was a real stereotype buster. The choice was made, in part, because thefts and pilfering by baggage handlers in UK airports has been on the rise. At Stansted Airport alone, 22 handlers have recently been arrested for stealing. British workers were being told that sending stray baggage to the country that gave rise to the Mafia offered passengers a better chance to get back their goods.

Ironically, Italy's flagship airline, Alitalia, is now on the edge of bankruptcy, while BAA/BA is looking at a price tag of around $32 million to pay for the world's worst baggage bungle. There are calls for the head of BA to resign. He's Irish by the way.

In the end, the software glitch may be patched, but this incident poses a rather haunting question about the London Summer Olympics of 2012. Many new buildings, facilities, and transport systems are being built in London to handle the anticipated crowds. The Conservative Party (Shadow) Transportation Secretary, Theresa Villers, has requested assurances from BA and BAA that Terminal Five matters will be straightened out in the next four years. The Olympic Torch -- now on its way to China -- was supposed to go through T-5, but that part of its London route was cancelled. Probably just as well. Both the Terminal and the Torch seem to have had very troubled journeys so far.

April 11, 2008

My Country Tis of Me

Mr. Obama, when you referred to your Grandmother as "a typical white person," I held my ire, but it got me thinking about grandparents and other mentors in one's life. When (as a theologian), I listened to the excerpts from Reverend Wright's sermons, I bit my lip until it bled. But then you went one step too far. You came after Pennsylvanians.

As anyone who has listened to the latest news cycles have learned, you described Pennsylvanians as being bitter, clinging to God and guns and anti-immigrant sentiments to do what psychologists call "transference."

That tipped my scales and sensibilities.

I have a message for you. As one does not mess with Texas, one ought also to beware of messing with Pennsylvanians.

One of my paternal Great Grandfathers arrived in Philadelphia in 1710.

Christian Juengling (or Yingling as the name became transliterated) produced eight children. Among his descendants are the famed architect, Norman Bel Geddes, and his famous daughter, Barbara, best know as Miss Ellie of Dallas. There are a host of us (less famous) descendants who have connected over the years. We hear from new ones all the time.

I learned about the depths of my Pennsylvanian roots when, just a few months before my paternal Grandmother died, a couple showed up on her doorstep. They had found her by using a 250-page Yingling family genealogy, written in 1957 by a distant cousin, Claude Rahn.

Grandmother's sister gave me contact info after Grandmother's funeral, in the early 1980's, and I was soon off on an ancestry recovery adventure.

We are an American story that you, Mr. Obama, do not get at all. My ancestors fought in the Revolutionary War -- with guns. We never owned slaves. We built churches. One still stands today in Trappe, Pennsylvania.

When Lutheran colonists reached a critical mass in Pennsylvania, the European Lutheran hierarchy sent Henry Melchoir Mulhenburg to organize the colonials. They had already begun to build schools to educate their own children and do other works of social import. My Great Grandfather was one of the men who built The Old Trappe Church. Mulhenburg worshiped there. I like to imagine he sat next to my Great Grandfather at some point.

In the 1990's, my husband and I served on a Cabinet of advisers to the President of the Lutheran Seminary in Gettysburg. It is inarguably the only seminary with actual canons on campus. These are remnants of the Civil War which is now remembered - via a high tech museum opened this very week in Gettysburg -- on what that battle meant to the preservation of the Union and the eventual abolition of slavery in America.

My branch of this Pennsylvanian family eventually made its way to Maryland. My parents met singing in a Lutheran church choir in Baltimore.

In 1968, after the murder of Martin Luther King, Jr., parts of Baltimore were going up in smoke. I still have the pass which allowed me to cross the police barrier -- on the county/city borderline - to get to the hospital where I was then in training as a nurse.

In 1969, still clinging to God, I integrated what had been -- until then -- an all Black college in Maryland - Morgan State. All Caucasian universities were being forced to integrate back then. Morgan was told that, unless it opened its doors to white students, it would lose funding which paid for Black kids to take extra courses designed to repair the gaps in their public (lesser) education. Convincing white kids to integrate Morgan at that juncture was a hard sell. Harvard and Princeton were a limited option for Black students at the time.

The Mother of a dear friend, a civil rights activist and loving woman, asked me to sign on as the first full time blond day student at Morgan, in January 1969. I did not hesitate. My Lutheran family did not stop me.

For their open-minded stance, the windows of my parent's home were regularly bombarded with eggs and fruit, and were sometimes broken.

Mr. Obama, if my family and I were typical white people - like your Grandmother - did our Pennsylvanian heritage make us "bitter?" I think not.

And may I ask, about what are we to be bitter? America still offers us all the same promise as it did our 18th century and subsequent ancestors, although big government often makes the paths to success more difficult. The immigrants whom you allege we hate are now a part of our family and we are proud (take note Mrs. Obama) to live in a blended world. We have intermarried with immigrant children from England, Scotland, Greece, and Pakistan, to name but a few countries. We say grace before meals. We contribute to our communities. We believe in America. We are not ashamed of it.

Your old paradigms are outdated, Mr. Obama. If you want to represent yourself as the leader of a new -- color neutral -- world order, you ought to look at the world which my family represents.

On the other hand, African American youth in the US drop out of high school at alarming rates. They have chosen to become a permanent underclass. They do not have hope-filled immigrant grandparents, nor apparently the right mentors. My Maternal Grandmother -- who arrived in America in 1910 from what is now

Slovakia -- could barely speak English, but her 13 children and their kids and their kids... all respect the values we were taught. We were expected to get to the library faithfully as soon as we could walk there on our own. Bill Cosby got it right.

Rather than preach against America, why didn't Rev. Wright mount a drive to get African American kids in Chicago to go to the library? How free are your cousins in Kenya to strive and choose to make a better world?

I have the impression that you are asking America to vote for some undefined change and, in the interim, to hold its collective breath until it all turns blue. Isn't it ironic that we have turned politics in the United States into a color divided (red state vs. blue state) proposition?

April 18, 2008

London's Mayoral Election Preview

The timing could not be more ironic. Tomorrow -- Thursday May 1, the once and possibly future most sacred day for Communists -- Londoners (including those who reside in its surrounding leafy green suburbs) will go to the polls. There being no Hillary equivalents on the ballot, they will be choosing among several men to determine who will be elected the Mayor of London, the second most powerful office in the UK.

It's a real horse race. The pollsters give the edge to Ken Livingstone, aka "Red" Ken. Looking for a third term, "Red" Ken is an unrepentant uber-leftist who used to mention Fidel Castro and Hugo Chavez in his campaign literature. He went so far left, the Labour Party disowned him years ago. Yet his eight-year reign as London's Mayor has not been ideological. It is more reminiscent of the old Daley machine in Chicago. Ken has raised cronyism to new heights.

For this and other reasons, England's betting shops favor Livingstone's opponent, the Oxford-educated Tory with a wild shock of blond hair, Boris Johnson, to win. So does The Gourmet Burger Kitchen at Tower Bridge which claims a near perfect record in predicting election outcomes. It reports that Boris Burgers are outselling Ken Burgers by almost two to one.

Running a distant third, it must be noted, is the candidate put up by the Liberal Democrats (the party left of plain old Labour). Brian Paddick is an openly gay former policeman, articulate and earnest, but he was not judged worthy of a listing on The Gourmet Burger menu. The English can be simultaneously eccentric -- and so judgmental.

Still, there is no getting round the meaty issues on the table in this election. Just a week ago, Livingstone admitted that he only submitted London as a host candidate for the 2012 Summer Olympics because he couldn't think of another way of extracting money from the populace to rehabilitate the East End and other bits of the City's creaking infrastructure. Before this stealth tax confession, Livingstone (born 17 June 1945) went public with the news that he had fathered a few children in previous (unmarried) relationships -- in addition to the toddlers he's had with his current young wife. The spin was that he's been a good Dad all along, however surreptiously. Very Kennedy-esque. Like New York's Mayor Bloomberg, Red Ken is known for taking the Underground (subway), although it's said no one pays much attention to him anymore when he does.

Perhaps this standoffish behavior comes from regular commuters who wish to have a bit of air conditioning on these subterranean saunas. It sometimes becomes so hot down the Tubes that the city sends paid public servants to hand out free bottles of water in an effort to prevent dehydration and strokes. Then there are the delays and price increases, not to mention the danger. Let's not forget the 7/7 suicide bombers who hit three Underground lines.

Boris Johnson has offered some ideas about improving public transport. He's promised to outlaw drinking on the Underground and the buses. Wow. Londoners are enthralled by the idea of not sitting (or standing in a human wedge) next to drunken footballers who often hurl (vomit) under these airless close contact conditions. Above ground, Johnson wants to take away the free (as in subsidized by taxes) city-issued transit passes from youths who bully their fellow passengers or trash the vehicles. Behave or pay your own way, says Boris. Very radical this Johnson fellow.

And he is somewhat of an odd duck. Alexander Boris de Pfeffel Johnson (born in New York City in 1964) is the grandson of a liberal Turkish Muslim journalist who was welcomed into Britain as a political refugee during World War 1. Boris made his mark as the editor of the conservative magazine, The Spectator, and has been a regular guest on British telly. Often portrayed as a buffoon by the media, Johnson was elected as the Member of Parliament for Henley. The town is famous for its yuppie population, gentrified residents, their piles (as aging mansions are known in England) and for rowing races on the river that runs through it. The Thames.

When the prospect of becoming Mayor of London surfaced, by all accounts, Johnson decided on a course of self-discipline. He found himself a stern group of advisers and put his Oxford education to work for him. Of late, he's taken to referring to his classical hero, Pericles, in campaign appearances. Pericles had quite lofty ideals about civil life and responsibilities in ancient Greece. Red Ken's response was to point out that Johnson never managed anything bigger than an influential (but limited circulation) conservative periodical, painting Boris as a sort of junior league William F. Buckley.

Red Ken has pulled out a few other campaign attack options. When it looked as if his fortunes were on the wane, he hired Barack Obama's political public relations people, Blue State Digital (and refuses to say what he's paid them). Boris has been using local talent, not out-sourcing.

There are other parallels between London's Mayoral contest and the US primary process. Red Ken and Boris have participated in 18 public debates. Last week, after their final TV interrogation, the sole BBC interviewer was rubbished over his treatment of Johnson, an echo of the Gibson/Stephanopoulos event on ABC. Religious issues have also surfaced. Livingston has taken heat for sharing a stage with a Muslim cleric, Yusuf Al- Qaradawi, a man who feels that wife beating and suicide bombings are (multi) culturally acceptable. This has pretty much assured Johnson will get the majority of votes from London's Jewish community. Based on his capricious re-routing of major city thoroughfares and his congestion (one pays up to £25/$50 to motor into Central London) charging scheme, Livingstone also cannot count on votes from car owners, nor from a single taxi driver. If you visit London, ask your driver for details.

Ken Livingstone has gratuitously offered Boris Johnson a job is he loses the election. But speculation has it that if Boris is victorious, he's an up-and-comer in the Tory Party. If so, he's already made that an uneasy career road for himself by asserting that he will face off against whoever is running the government if he thinks Londoners are being ill-served. Insiders forecast a nail biting (up-all-night) vote count. There will be no hanging chads, but the winner may not be decided until well into May 2. With the fortunes of Gordon Brown and the Labour Party on a serious decline, a Tory takeover of England's capitol city could presage David Cameron's rise as the next Prime Minister by the summer of 2010.

Boris and the Torries Trounce Labour

The ballots were still being counted on Friday May 2 -- and it was far from a landslide - (53 to 46 %) albeit a record turnout of voters. But by noon, the bookies had already declared Boris Johnson the new Mayor of London. Appropriately enough, May 2 is the day on the Orthodox Church calendar that honors Saint Boris of Bulgaria. Post-election comments -- penned in the daily newspapers from assorted left leaning grumblers, snidely suggested that it would take at least one saint (or a collection of them, plus a bevy of guardian angels) to keep Boris from dragging London down to a new level of hell.

Meanwhile, over at Number 10 Downing Street, Prime Minister Gordon Brown's single working brown eye was turning blue and possibly weeping. He was reading the election results from across the United Kingdom and the news for Labour was devastating. It was the Party's worst showing in 40 years. More than 300 council seats were lost. 240 of those seats went to Conservative candidates, with significant gains made in the North Country and in Wales. The Tories garnered 46 percent of the votes. By comparison, only 23 percent of the public voted for Labour placing that party in third place behind the Liberal Democrats who received 24 percent of the national votes.

These results were a reverse image of Labour's victory, in 1995, under Tony Blair's leadership. Tongues wagged when a photo of a beaming Blair was snapped outside a chic Mayfair eatery on election night. Blair knew that Brown would be a disaster as PM and held off leaving office as long as possible. His Cheshire Cat grin purred out: 'told you so' to Labourites and to critics who accused him of clinging to power.

Ever the dour Scot, Brown blamed "difficult economic circumstances" for this terrible ballot bashing, assuring the citizens that the Government's plans to address these circumstances would become a bit more clear "over the next few months." Too little too late, was the reply. Polls indicate that only 32 percent of the public have confidence in the economy. Less than half of the country feels Mr. Brown is competent. When an election is called, no later than 2010, the betting shops are already giving the odds to another Tory sweep and that means David Cameron will become the next Prime Minister. (Please note: Explaining how the British parliamentary system works requires a meaty essay, a dictionary of terms and at least mild inebriation).

Much of this rosy outlook for a future Conservative Party ascent to power depends on how Boris Johnson handles his new job. He will be the canary in the coal mine, a political cliché not lost on the Welsh.

Johnson and David Cameron go back 25 years, to their days as students at Eton and Oxford, two of England's ultimate old boy's educational clubs. Boris was thought to be a clever Classics student. Cameron less so, but more earnest. Rumor has it that Cameron called Johnson about his run for Mayor, but made him vow to clean up his act so the Tories would not be embarrassed by his notorious antics and boisterous sense of humor. Past episodes include Boris having once referred to black children as "picanninies" in a Spectator Magazine article. He also managed to insult the residents of Liverpool and dissed one of the UK's most popular TV chefs. He apologized for the first of these indiscretions, but took the blows on Liverpool and the chef.

To assure Cameron of his sincerity, Johnson gave up drinking for three months. This fact was revealed in a TV interview given by Johnson's Father, Stanley, a lively and engaging man in his own right. The elder Johnson shared family photos which do prove the family are descended from natural blond Turks. As reported here last week, Johnson's grandfather -- born Osman Ali -- was a Turkish journalist and (briefly) a minister in to the Grand Vizier of the Ottoman Empire. Osman, a Muslim, relocated to England just after World War One and changed his name to Wilfred Johnson. Boris points out that since his wife's Mother is from India, their four children are truly multi-ethnic so he cannot be accused of cultural insensitivity. Demographically, this is important as one in every six London voters are from an ethnic minority - the largest and wealthiest of these being from Indian backgrounds. They own an estimated 10,000 businesses in greater London.

Johnson's management insensitivities are another matter. He has no credentials in this arena. To that end, Cameron's people are making sure that the best and the brightest available Tories surround Boris. For his part, Johnson (who was sworn into office on Saturday morning -- the 3rd) promised to "work flat out from now on to earn your trust and dispel some of the myths that have been created about me."

True to his word, Johnson met immediately with the Metropolitan Police Commissioner, Sir Ian Blair (no relation to Tony). He told England's most senior law enforcement officer that if London's crime statistics are not dramatically and quickly improved, Blair could expect to be fired. Although Johnson has made conciliatory comments about his predecessor, Ken Livingstone, pledging to build on Red Ken's achievements as Mayor, the new Mayor's incoming staff has been instructed to go through the file cabinets and archives to look for evidence of corruption under Livingstone's regime.

Johnson quipped: "I imagine there are shredding machines quietly puffing and panting away in various parts of the building . . . Heaven knows what we shall uncover in the course of the next few days." To sore losers in the Labour Party who try to make trouble for the victorious Tories, the new Mayor promised: "If there are any dogs in the manger, then I will have those dogs humanely euthanased."

With Johnson's ability to run London in question -- especially with the 2012 Summer Olympics on his plate -- Boris has already made a characteristically pre-emptive self-deprecating joke. He says that if he does well, he might like to run for President of the United States someday. He is (technically) Constitutionally eligible to do just that as he was born in New York City. Of course, he'd have to reapply to renew his recently relinquished American citizenship.

May 5, 2008

Gordon Brown's British Speed Bumps

At the risk of sounding like actress Sharon Stone (who recently opined that the earthquake in China was cosmic retribution for its treatment of Tibet), one simply has to say that Prime Minister Gordon Brown is the poster boy for bad karma. Whatever he does seems to cause the earth to roil and rumble beneath his feet.

In a mid-May election to replace a dead MP, the Labor Party lost a long held Labor seat in a Tory landslide. The long knives within the Labor Party (already sharpened to a fine edge and ready to slay the bungling head of their Party) came out again. This time, they were used only to point to Brown's continually dismal performance as Prime Minister.

No one wanted to actually stab the Labor Party leader (or see him assassinated), but the media relentlessly gossiped about secret meetings and plans to whittle down the length of Brown's reign. Likewise, Brown is rumored to have countered with threat. Should the Party attempt to remove him from office, he was presumably prepared to respond with a scorched earth policy. This was made known in conjunction with the release of a trial balloon. It was hinted that Brown might name a Deputy Prime Minister, an unidentified figure whose charisma and public appeal might buffer Brown's hangdog persona and plummeting public approval ratings.

Most frequently named as a candidate for the Deputy PM position was David Milliband, currently serving as the Foreign Secretary. According to sources, Milliband was the man Cherie Blair favored to replace her husband, Tony, as Prime Minister. Alas, Cherie has a new autobiography out which has caused teeth to grind and howls to be sent up to heaven, so any hint that Milliband was her choice is bound to be held against him.

But back to Tibet...Proving he was incapable of doing the diplomatic side-step, on the heels of the dismal by-election results, Brown met with the Dalai Lama across the Thames from the Houses of Parliament in Lambeth Palace, the official digs of the Archbishop of Canterbury in London. The idea was to avoid provoking the wrath of China by not welcoming the titular head of Tibet into Number Ten Downing Street. Although they were distracted by the aftermath of that terrible and tragic earthquake, the Chinese still managed to protest about Brown and the Lama having a chat at all.

In the high irony department, word leaked out about what was said between the spiritual leader and the PM. It seems the Dalai Lama told Brown that one should not overlook the lessons that failures provide in life. Good advice indeed for a man who has whatever one calls the opposite of "the golden touch."

Take Brown's actual track record in that very commodity. In 1999, when he was serving as Chancellor of the Exchequer, Gordon Brown announced that he intended to sell off more than half of England's gold reserves -- 400 tons. His decision was reportedly based on the observation that the price of gold had remained static for more than a decade. Brown went ahead with the sale against the advice of officials within the Bank of England, which had successfully managed England's gold reserves for 300 years. The gold bullion sold -- in a total of 17 auctions -- for an average of $275 an ounce. This became known among gold dealers as the "Brown Bottom" of the market. Today, gold is selling for between $900 and $1000 per ounce. By selling the 400 tons in 1999, instead of 2008, Brown lost the country around $8 billion in profits. At the same time, he wrecked the retirement funds for a whole generation of British workers.

The then Chancellor Brown spent the next 18 months trying to keep the press from going public with the story of how he ignored the advice of the Bank of England. This gives new depth to the metaphor of a politician having "a tin ear."

Back in the present, Brown was greeted, on Tuesday May

27th, with a blockade of London roads spanning both morning and evening commute times. About 1000 angry lorrie (truck) drivers rolled their rigs into the capital city to protest rising fuel prices. One small trucker explained that he owned five trucks that only got 6 to 8 miles per (Imperial) gallon. Current diesel petrol prices have driven up the cost of fueling his business to £3000 ($6000) per week. Some truckers say they can only remain in business under these conditions until the fall. This translates into the breakdown of delivery mechanisms for goods within the UK and the loss of thousands of jobs.

In response to this convoy of consternation, Brown announced that he would -- first -- talk with OPEC -- and would also urge oil producers in the North Sea to increase production and, while he was at it, would press for increased development of nuclear power. But experts say that additional oil from the North Sea would do little or nothing to impact petrol supplies, and the nuclear option is at least a decade away.

But it was a good ploy to distract the press from the fact that the UK Treasury's petrol tax take has doubled in just over a year. And in a down-the-rabbit-hole-Alice moment, the Secretary of Transport went on the BBC to suggest that people should sell their inefficient and fuel guzzling cars and buy new more eco-friendly models. When pressed, he was unable to explain who would buy all those gas-guzzlers and how this sort of automotive shuffle was going to do anything at all to solve the immediate problem. In a corollary move, Brown was forced to scrap plans to impose a "green tax" on millions of family cars. This idea fostered a near revolt of what was left of Brown's support, as the tax would have hit middle and lower middle classes the hardest. For a Laborite, this is the equivalent of the most unforgivable sin, along the lines of all the things George W. Bush has done to deconstruct conservatism and risk the downfall of the Republican Party.

Brown is so desperate to regain popularity, he's now cold-calling British voters at home. ("Oo is it Maudie?" "It's that pest Brown again. Do you want to tell 'im to bugger off this time, or shall I?")

Isn't it curious that just as the Tories (still identified by the color blue) are resurgent in England, the Republican Party of America has acquiesced to being identified by the color red (long associated with communism). In 1984, Reagan's re-election was reported on TV as "a sea of blue" on the American electoral map. This color shift purportedly was the handiwork of the late Peter Jennings of ABC, Canada's socialist gift to media America. And it stuck. Now the only thing blue about US conservatives is their mood.

June 2, 2008

The Mouse That Roared

The result of Ireland's crucial vote on the "New Europe" Lisbon Treaty was announced on Friday the 13th. The Irish said NO! despite a rare moment of consensus which saw all three of Eire's political parties campaigning for a YES vote. From modest cajoling to guilt to dire warnings and outright threats, no ploy was left unplayed. It didn't work.

Brussels bureaucrats -- who have been busy designing the European Union as a perpetual source of power and job security for themselves and future generations of political hacks - could scarcely believe it. A mouse -- albeit a mighty free-market-oriented one on the rise - had roared. In denial, EU spokespeople kept saying that this was not the end; that their dream of empire had not been dealt a fatal blow.

But the facts say otherwise.

This "new Europe" -- version 5.0 -- had a humble beginning in the post-WWII early 50's as the innocent-enough European Steel and Coal Board. This morphed into the European Economic Community, a broader free-trade-zone for the nascent European continental powers. By the mid-80's, with the edition of Great Britain, newer treaties created the European Community, expanding political as well as economic ties. Finally, yet another treaty signed in Maastrecht in the early 90's established the European Union, Mark IV version, the current model which has created the Euro, border-free movement and a rotating presidency hosted every 6 months by one of the now 27-strong EU member countries.

But somewhere along the way, the EU ceased to represent the interests of its nations' people as the desire for "ever closer union" was pushed by the unelected Eurocrats. Back in 2005, an all-reaching "European Union Constitution" was proposed. It would create a new EU President, Foreign Minister, army, and virtually veto-free bureaucracy to which all member states would be subservient. It would supersede all the previous treaties.

Unfortunately for the Eurocrats (but fortunately for European freedom), it was rejected by voters in France and the Netherlands, resulting in other countries cancelling their scheduled ratification votes. Undaunted by this initial rejection, the pro-EU forces took the core of the Constitution and using reconstructive surgery inserted the guts of the discredited treaty into the dozen existing treaties, reintroducing the document as "The Lisbon Reform Treaty".

In this second go-round, Brussels opted to use the stealth factor. This time, voters wouldn't be allowed to have a say. Only governments -- acting directly -- would approve the surrender of national governance to the EU.

If voters in the EU's 27 member states would not affirm their massive bureaucratic plan for domination, then allowing people to vote at all would have to be removed as an obstacle.

Britain's ruling Labour Party (under both Tony Blair and now Gordon Brown) had promised that there would be a citizen's referendum on the Treaty, just as they had previously promised a vote on what became the failed Constitution. Both promises were broken. Instead, Gordon Brown snuck off to an EU meeting in Portugal last year and signed off on the "Reform Treaty" when he thought no one was looking.

Such utter disregard for the wishes of the people has been cited as a sign that the once hallowed British system of laws and rights is being systematically dismantled. So much for the Magna Carta.

The same process was at work in the other 17 countries which have also ratified the new Treaty without conducting popular votes. This included France and the Netherlands -- whose populations would not be permitted to make the same mistake twice.

By Sunday morning, June 15, Downing Street was awash with rumors. It was hinted that Gordon Brown was now inclined to "do a 180" and "sacrifice" the Lisbon Treaty, letting it collapse under its own dead weight. It was said he could see the pro and con Treaty forces pulling Europe into a two-tiered, or two-speed, economic system in Europe - one in which the UK would likely be relegated to the second tier.

The Irish have had a different and more turbulent history and are now on the other (brighter) side of their long dark tunnel of turmoil.

Eire's economy -- the "Celtic tiger" -- is booming. The nation's success is in large part due to its business-friendly taxes, which encourage corporations to locate there. This, in turn, has created significant numbers of new jobs and brought an eager generation of young people – from across Europe - into the Irish workforce. Contrast this to aging populations in decline – such as one finds in Germany. Their social programs will eventually run dry for lack of enough young people to fund the ongoing retirement load. The Irish, a nation of well-educated young people, want no part of this socialist burden.

Over the weekend, analysts, editorialists, and bloggers in the UK media reflected the views of their counterparts across Europe.

Free-market conservatives like Vaclav Klaus, President of the Czech Republic declared the Treaty "finished". "Ratification cannot be continued," he said, and. called the Irish vote "a victory of freedom and reason over artificial elitist projects and European Bureaucracy".

One repeatedly cited problem -- from both pro and con sides -- was that the 350-page plus Treaty was never properly explained to voters. The result was that anti-Treaty factions were suspicious and pro-Treaty advocates claimed their agenda was not sufficiently articulated.

Frank-Walter Steinmeier, Germany's foreign minister, went further, stating that the Lisbon treaty provisions could be implemented without Ireland -- a slap in the face of democracy.

But on the other side, Emmanuel Bordez, of the Mouvement Pour La France Party said "People feel despised and cheated by their leaders,"

In an editorial, Italy's Republica questioned: "Is it possible to reach 50 (the EU's age) without knowing where you belong? Is it forbidden to investigate why?"

The Austrian Der Standard wrote: "The zero hour is bringing the chance of a new start. Brussels and the governments of EU-countries must finally understand that the citizens do not want an EU where everything is decided in Brussels."

A summit of the current EU leaders convenes on this coming Thursday where they will be looking for "possible solutions to the crisis generated by the Irish no vote". French President Sarkozy , who will take over the rotating EU presidency next month, dismissed the Irish vote as but a "hiccup" that should "not become a political crisis".

The implicit threat to real democracy is that the EU powers-that-be will continue to propose variations on an EU Constitution until they achieve their desired results -- even if it means goose-steeping over the wishes of Europe's 500 million people. As one observer questioned, "What part of 'No' don't you understand?"

June 16, 2008

Emperor Sarkozy Conquers the Mediterranean

Nicholas Sarkozy – who began his six-month turn as Acting President of the European Union on July 1st - is in a position of power that Napoleon would have envied. Being in the catbird seat of the EU is just the half of it.

In early 2007, when he was campaigning to become the President of France, Sarkozy floated a grandiose idea. He said that if elected he would create a grand alliance consisting of the 21 countries, on three continents, which border the Mediterranean Sea. This new political entity, he vowed, would enrich the lives of the 400 million residents in those 21 countries, bringing Christians, Jews, and Muslims together as never before to solve regional issues, and perhaps end conflicts in the Middle East for one and for all. This was all seen as very ambitious since the functional realities of constructing this proposed alliance were unformed back then. This is now. Sarkozy is proving to be the energizer bunny of world politics with - his detractors fret - a tendency toward megalomania.

On July 14th, 2008, Bastille Day (France's Independence Day equivalent), Sarkozy publicly christened his cherished political baby, the Union for the Mediterranean.

Developed by way of something known as "The Barcelona Process," Sarko's Mediterranean Union (quickly dubbed "Club Med" by the European media) now supposedly binds together not 21, but 43 member countries, with a combined population of 800 million, some of which are nowhere near the Mediterranean Sea.

This new entity came into being on the heels of the Irish NO vote on the failed European Union Constitution (aka the Lisbon Treaty), an act of rebellion greeted by Sarko with contempt. He glowered and declared that the Irish would just have to vote again. He delivered himself of this opinion on Irish soil no less. This got the leader of Sinn Fein, very riled up and that could be a plot for novelist Tom Clancy down the line if those risky fences aren't mended.

But on Bastille Day, everything seemed rosy. Sarkozy and his new glamorous, top of the pop charts, one time nude model wife, Carla Bruni, beamed as parachutists filtered down from the skies above Paris, while smartly dressed military troops marched down the Champs Elysees. In the reviewing stands for the big show were Israel's scandal-ridden Prime Minister Ehud Olmert, Syria's President Bashar al-Assad, Egyptian President Hosni Mubarak, Lebanon's new President Michel Suleiman, Prime Minister Erdogan of Turkey, Palestine's Mahmoud Abbas, as well as representatives from Morocco, Algeria, Jordan, Greece and Cyprus, plus delegates from the 27 existing EU member states, and a few folks from the Balkans. 18,000 French police were required to provide security for this collection of strange bedfellows. The only no-show was Libya's Muammar Gaddafi, who is skeptical about the whole idea. He is not alone.

Early on, Germany let it be known that it was not happy about having EU funds redirected to finance Club Med. Chancellor Angela Merkel (who is no fan of Sarko) suspected he was out to create northern and southern spheres of influence, taking the latter for himself. Sarkozy did little to discourage Merkel's worries when he announced that the initial meetings of Club Med's charter members would be run by him, with Egypt's Mubarak serving as "co-presider." Mubarak is no spring chicken and is unlikely to take any of the limelight away from Sarkozy. However, other voices from the southern contingent are already accusing the European states of dominating them. And the ink isn't even dry on the membership cards.

Some other questions have surfaced. Do Europeans need yet another super bureaucracy to suck up their money and run even more of their lives? Wasn't Brussels enough already? How much trust and commonweal can be expected between Brussels and the Middle East? What can a committee of 43 members actually accomplish when their cultures, economies and interests are so diverse? Does Sarkozy want the Nobel Peace Prize, or is he just doing an Oprah?

Sarkozy was quoted as saying Club Med summits offered members the chance to learn how to love one another. Or is he planning to create a new world order monocracy with himself in the role of monarch? Only time will tell.

Six preliminary goals were agreed to by all parties in the initial meetings held before the July 14th pomp and glory display. These are: cleaning up the Mediterranean Sea, developing a Mediterranean Solar Energy Plan, developing better maritime and land highways, setting up joint civil protection and disaster response plans, creating a Euro-Mediterranean University as part of a greater Euro Mediterranean Higher Education and Science Research Institute and the creation of an overall Mediterranean Business Development Initiative.

Once again, very ambitious, especially since the foreign ministers of the Club members will only meet once a year, with a general summit called every two years. Who runs what and which "secretariat" (a term that makes everyone outside the horseracing world slightly nervous) will be placed in what country is all up for discussion. It is troubling that immigration matters were brushed aside to create an aura of harmony. Yes, it all seems impossibly idealistic, and brings Woodrow Wilson to mind. The difference is that Sarkozy is a driven man, so it could all be fun to watch. Or frightening.

Speaking of fun things to watch, Barack Obama will visit President Sarkozy at the Elysee Palace - on July 25th - as part of his European pre-victory tour. Afterwards, the dynamite duo will hold a joint press conference. Having seen recent photos of tall skinny Obama playing B Ball at the gym, and thinking of the diminutive Sarkozy, one cannot wait to see how the press gets both of these guys in the same frame without resorting to special effects.

July 24, 2008

The Canterbury Travails

On August 3rd, Rowan Williams, the archbishop of Canterbury, released a statement at the end of the Lambeth Conference urging the Church's hierarchy not to consecrate any more openly gay bishops. Held once every ten years, the Lambeth Conference is a meeting of all bishops serving in the worldwide Anglican Communion and derives its name from the Palace of Lambeth, the official London residence of the ABC. In Williams' summary remarks, he also petitioned the 77 million members of Anglican Communion -- which includes the U.S. Episcopal Church -- to give its leaders "further space for study and free discussion without pressure" on matters of human sexuality.

The space to which Williams refers opened up first in 1992, when the Church of England (HQ for the Anglican Communion) began ordaining women as priests. This resulted in a mini-exodus of male traditionalists who contended that Jesus only wanted men in leadership positions. Taking its own counsel, the Episcopal Church forced the issue. It began independently ordaining women bishops and eventually elected a woman as its national Presiding Bishop. When the dust cleared at Lambeth, a resolution was passed which will now allow women to become bishops throughout the worldwide Communion. That put a high hurdle in the Anglican-Catholic dialogue, but Rowan Williams and Co. no longer risk being labeled as "misogynists." The sexuality hurdle has proved insurmountable at present.

In 2003, the Episcopal Church consecrated Gene Robinson as a bishop in New Hampshire. Robinson's elevation was met with grievances on two points. Not only was he openly gay and living in a same sex relationship, Robinson was a divorced father of two. It was said by his detractors that this man obviously has trouble keeping solemn vows. Once the blessings of same sex unions was also put on the theological table, the betting odds went up that a schism was inevitable.

In the world of religious institutions, schism (from the Greek schisma) refers to the rupture of an ecclesiastical union. The two big ones that come easily to mind are Martin Luther's 15th century Protestant Reformation and Henry the 8th's divorce, in the 16th century, which led to the creation of the (Anglican) Church of England. Over the centuries, there have been many smaller schisms out of which new church bodies were formed. But tremors along the Anglican fault lines seemed to suggest this could be another big one. Could an open rebellion be forestalled? The answer turned out to be "yes," but only just.

For a start, 230 of the serving 900 Anglican Bishops on the planet boycotted the Lambeth. Conference. A goodly portion of those absent serve as Bishops in African countries, where the Church is actually growing in size and influence. They protested that if the Church adopted pro-gay policies, it would be harder for them to compete for souls against Islam -- a religion that completely rejects homosexuality. The Africans are also fighting the AIDS epidemic and feel that Church-directed strict moral practices are an essential component of their battle against the spread of this disease. Although he has spoken out against anti-gay violence, the Anglican primate of Nigeria, Dr. Peter Akinola, has endorsed the Nigerian government's recent plans to strengthen laws against homosexuality, and so he forbade his bishops to attend the conference. Only one bishop, Cyril Okorocha of Owerri, broke ranks and flew to England. Akinola has become a figurehead in the revolt against the liberal wing of the Church. He has encouraged congregations to break away from their local liberal-minded dioceses. In the U.S., 100 Episcopal parishes (of 7000 nationwide) have already taken this path.

Voicing the opposing view is Integrity, the advocacy group for gay and lesbian Episcopalians. Integrity's position is that "there is no theological defense for sacrificing a minority of the baptized for the sake of unity." The group asserts that one day the Church will regret its treatment of gays and lesbians as it came to regret supporting slavery in the past. Pro-gay advocates were filled with ire by the news that Robinson had been deliberately left off the Lambeth invitation list. Robinson flew to England on his own and maintained a visible presence, giving interviews to members of the banished media.

What banished media, you ask? Another tactic the ABC used to manage the proceedings was to draw up a list of unfriendly media people, relegating them to a "press room" way "off-campus." This led several of the ostracized group to comment that the ABC had acquired "the Stalinist touch." The outcasts delighted in running with stories from other dissidents. Howls of official outrage ensued after a U.S. woman bishop gave an interview in which she claimed some bishops probably beat their wives, especially those from countries where wife beating was culturally acceptable. An African bishop called in to excoriate the Anglicans for being a relic of British colonialism. This generated heated retorts about how the Africans ought to do more to stop genocides in their own backyards.

But it wasn't all without a bit of fun. Before the serious talks got underway, the Bishop of Columbo, Sri Lanka, suggested the liberals and conservatives form teams and settle their dispute by playing a cricket match. The spiritual entertainment was very ecumenical. One Canterbury service featured Buddhist chants and grass-skirted native Melanesian dancers. For exercise, the bishops were handed picket signs bearing the message: "Do Justice -- Love Mercy," and were organized to walk -- with representatives of other faiths -- around London. Then there were the surprised looks when discussion groups were handed directions on how to employ a method of conflict resolution pioneered by the Zulus.

Curiously, the Vatican sent its largest delegation ever to Lambeth --13 in all. Their assignment was to "help impose discipline and unity." A Dominican friar, an Italian monk, and a Catholic cardinal acted as sort of personal support trio for the Archbishop of Canterbury. As one religion reporter quipped, Rowan Williams knew he was facing a family feud, so he called in some distant relatives from Italy to keep things under control. The Catholics were also on hand in case things blew up, ready to welcome any Anglicans who wanted to return to the Mother Church. Indeed, 100 Anglican parishes in the UK have already begun exploring a way to transfer their churches to Team Rome. Alas, Ivan Dias, the attending cardinal, put the wind up a few purple vestments when he said that the Anglican Church is "suffering from spiritual Alzheimer's and ecclesial Parkinson's."

The Vatican presence is credited with influencing the most unexpected decision to come out of Lambeth. A Faith and Order Commission, along the lines of the Vatican's own Congregation for the Doctrine of the Faith, has been created. Anglican bishops will now begin to write down a code of common law for their church, similar to the Roman Catholic Code of Canon. This action was met with deep concern and nervousness. The Bishop of New York observed that the genius of Anglicanism is that is hasn't codified too many things, to which the Bishop of Lincoln added: "People complain that we do not know who we are but part of what it means to be Anglican is not being able to say precisely who we are."

Confusing? Yes, and that is the Lambeth legacy in a nutshell. Rowan Williams got his study time extension, but chances are he'll be gone in ten years anyway when the next Bishop's conference convenes. He dodged the schism, but the church-within-a-church Communion truce is unlikely to heal or hold. And now he has bishops worried that Anglicans are going to be forced to write down precisely who they are and what they stand for. In a post-Lambeth survey, 75% of participants reported being satisfied with the current Archbishop of Canterbury, but a third indicated the Anglican Church has never been in worse shape.

For those who wish to see an end to organized religion, this must come as good news.

August 6, 2008

Bedlam in Britain: Outlaws and Disorder

The word "bedlam" derives from the popular nickname bestowed on the Hospital of St. Mary of Bethlehem in London. It was -- in politically incorrect but descriptive terms -- a lunatic asylum in which deplorable conditions were the norm. On a sliding fee basis, the public could view the poor souls confined there, poke them with sticks for fun, and even have sex with them. Thus "bedlam" is now synonymous shorthand for "a scene or state of uproar and confusion."

A quick scan of news stories on the Labour government's recent scandals and antics makes it clear that not much has changed in London since the 19th century. Bedlam prevails.

This includes staggering evidence that the British government has been suffering from a serious case of reverse kleptomania. Last week, Liberal Democrat MP Sarah Teather announced the results of an investigation she has been conducting. Since 2001, Teather discovered, government departments have registered the loss -- or theft -- of a total of 3,200 laptop computer and mobile phones. This works out to 468 devices per year, or more than one per day. Many of the laptops contained what is considered "sensitive information."

Thus, no one should be surprised by this second incomprehensible news item from last week. An unencrypted data stick went missing from the offices of a consulting company hired by The Home Office. What was on the stick? Would you believe confidential information on the 84,000 prisoners (now serving time) in England and Wales and 43,000 individuals (now back on the streets) described as "prolific and serious offenders" who have repeatedly committed violent and/or sexual crimes?

This was not the first database to disappear during Gordon

Brown's reign as Prime Minister. Last year, the private records of 25 million UK children who receive government health benefits, the names of people who had applied for driving learner's permits, and -- incredulously -- the names of new Army recruits, also went missing. New security procedures were promised, but obviously not delivered.

And now for the gallow's humor. The public has been told that one of the possible consequences of the missing data stick is that criminals could bring legal actions against the government if their identities and home addresses are revealed and they are placed in danger. This is known as "toxic liability" and, should such suits occur, the government says compensation and damages will have to be paid for through increased taxes. The good news is that PA Consulting has had its other government contract put on hold for now. That would be the contract to develop government issued Identity Cards for every citizen in the UK.

Another lavishly funded British government contract involves the redesign and manufacture of unmanned spy aircraft (drones -- not be to confused by bureaucrats) currently being used in Afghanistan and Iraq. The plan is to have these drones deployed domestically across the length and breadth of the UK to monitor ordinary citizens. As one indignant Brit exclaimed: "We won't be able to sunbathe in the nude in our own back gardens anymore." The drones are scheduled to be flying and spying within the next three years.

Speaking of spies, MI5 -- aka The British Security Service -- just announced a new recruitment program designed to entice gays and lesbians to join their ranks. This new policy upends the anti-gay hiring ban established in the 1950s, when two gay Cambridge students (Guy Burgess and Anthony Blunt) created a notoriously successful Cold War Pro-Soviet spy ring. The decision was based on the increased need for intelligence officers following the 7/7 terrorist bombings in London. To achieve its hiring goals, MI5 has outsourced to a gay and lesbian recruitment firm named Stonewall. A spokesperson for MI5 explained: "People from all minority communities do have experience of getting on with people who are different and of fitting in. They are also good at doing these things in a way that is not conspicuous." The obvious questions are how many gay and lesbian Islamic extremists are in England, and just how likely are they to get on inconspicuously with these new MI5 recruits?

But back to domestic surveillance. As if the wall-to-wall CCTV cameras across the low and high streets of the British Isles were not sufficient, a new plan has been proffered which calls for hidden CCTV cameras to be installed in the nation's schools. The initial reaction of the Association of Teachers and Lecturers was mixed, but only 25 percent expressed concern over this new level of intrusion. 50 percent of ATL members said they didn't think CCTV in classrooms would make any difference in how they taught their classes, although they might feel safer from attacks from rowdy students.

Another headline of note reported that London is now one of the most dangerous places in Britain in the wake of a spate of murders. Since 2008 began, 24 teenagers have been stabbed to death in the capital. Sadly, the "top cop" of London's Metropolitan Police Department has been distracted lately. Sir Ian Blair (no relation to Tony) was nearly fired in 2005 when a squad of his men mistook a Brazilian electrician for a terrorist and shot the man to death in an Underground station. Now Blair is preoccupied with a lawsuit -- brought against him by Scotland Yard's highest-ranking Muslim officer -- who claims he is the object of job discrimination.

But all is not lost. Seems the coppers in County Kent have their priorities straight. They recently seized a satirical War on Terror board game created by two web designers from Cambridge University. Why? Some players have to wear a ski mask (balaclava) with the word "Evil" stitched on it. The police said the bust was executed because these masks could be used in the commission of actual crimes. The game's creators believe that the real reason they were targeted was that their game allowed for several scenarios in which the axis of evil empires could win the war on terror, roundly defeating the good empires. It's increasingly hard to ignore that possibility.

Surveying the bedlam, Nick Clegg, leader of the Liberal Democrat Party, told the press last week: "Charlie Chaplin could do a better job of running the Home Office than this Labour government."

August 28, 2008

European Press More Skeptical of Obama than Ours

As the Democrat's convention week dawned, The Times of London ran a curious headline: "Barack Obama prepares for his flamboyant tilt at the White House." The mind's eye blinked a bit trying to visualize someone executing a "flamboyant tilt."

Reporting for The Times from Denver, Tom Baldwin and Tim Reid launched their Convention Diary by observing: "Somewhere in the midst of all the razzamatazz, security scares and psycho babble about The Clintons' state of mind, Barack Obama has an important message. The trouble, say some worried Democrats, is that it is not getting through." To illustrate the ugly reality behind attempts to choreograph a show of party unity, Baldwin and Reid quoted Jesse Jackson Jr.'s lament that the wounds from the nomination battle had become infected with a "little bit of pus." Ouch. Conversely they described the scene in the Pepsi Center as "part theme park gift shop and part sales conference" and seemed amused that "every 20 minutes or so, a live band strikes up and everybody gets up to dance or wave their placards."

Gerard Baker, U.S. editor for The Times, acknowledged that "speech-making is what Sen. Obama does best," but he went on to wonder if that same soaring rhetoric could also bring him down. Baker explained: "His very ability to move audiences with words and dramatic set-piece performances is now part of the principal critique of him by his opponents: that he is a profoundly inexperienced young man who has done no more in his short public life than give great speeches. The more he inspires and moves his followers with great speeches the more glaring the gap between his speaking talent and his callowness appears."

The UK liberal leaning New Statesman Magazine, arguably pro-Obama on political grounds, proclaimed "Obama Comes Out Fighting," but it was very hard on the handling of the Invesco Pageant. The Stateman's reporter, Andrew Stevens, revealed that 20,000 more tickets were handed out than there were seats in the stadium. This was done to make sure that the 80,000 seats were filled for Obama's speech, but it left many disgruntled people waiting in lines for a very long time with a number ultimately being turned away.

Stevens characterized this as "thoroughly political and highly calculated." He was also put off by certain media people's abandoning any hint of impartiality as exemplified by CNN's main anchorman "getting up and dancing -- off camera -- with an Obama strategist." As for the acceptance speech, Stevens labeled it "a shopping list of all the positive things an Obama administration would deliver."

The purpose-driven acceptance staging of The Invesco Center event became a target for many a wry remark, especially when news leaked out that the same folks did the set for Brittany Spears' last concert. Once it was seen on TV, the Greek Temple analogies were dropped in favor of snappier fare like "The Mile High West Wing." One panoramic newspaper photo of Sen. Obama delivering his speech, with his image looming large on screens to either side of him, bore the caption: "Barack Obama can play an already compliant audience like the proverbial violin."

Several articles pondered the custom of inviting the wives of candidates to give speeches at Party conventions. This is simply not done in either Britain or Europe. It is laughable to them. Simon Heffer of the Telegraph suggested that this indicates America has -- ironically -- become entranced by the idea of having a family on the throne. "We have had the Bush family ad nauseum, the Kennedys ditto -- with old Ted yanked from his sickbed to endorse Mr. Obama in a stunt that made On Golden Pond seem light on sentimentality." How, the European press wondered, could so many people fall for this kind of Hollywood hype?

Gabor Steingart, writing in Germany's Der Spiegel, said that it would be a mistake to assume the throngs who listened to Obama's speech in Berlin agreed with what he said, describing the Senator's campaign as "a romantic revolution." Steingart explained that there is a vast difference in Europe between "romantic democrats" and those with common sense. Steingart then listed all of the promises Obama made in his acceptance speech and said "it's possible to be impressed by all this -- or to find it shameless."

Horst Teltschik, a former adviser to former Chancellor Helmut Kohl, assessed Obama's Berlin appearance as ambivalent because it was unlikely that a German politician would draw such a big crowd at the Washington Monument. He added: "His opponent, John McCain, has been coming to Germany every year for decades. He knows all the most important politicians personally."

The UK Telegraph's reporter, Tim Shipman, closed out his convention diary with a religious round-up under the headline: "Barack Obama's Messiah complex and other tricky questions." Shipman quoted an unnamed Democrat strategist as saying that Obama had not gone far enough in proclaiming himself "The One," laying into the candidate for being wishy washy at the faith forum when he said that conception and abortion questions were above his pay grade. The Dem exclaimed, "The President of the United States is God. He's more God than God. He can kill six billion people, just like that, by pressing a button. Unless there's a major Biblical plague, God doesn't get close." This ought to prove that there is unquestionably a religious left with an evangelically apocalyptic wing.

Because of time zone differences, the news of Sarah Palin becoming John McCain's running mate did not get a full press court until the late news cycles in Europe. The BBC homepage story headline was short and sweet: "McCain Unveils 'The Barracuda.'"

The Palin decision was preliminarily deemed either risky or brilliant. Everyone scrambled for 18 hours to get up to speed. By Sunday, The Times had a different spin. It ran a photo of the attractive Governor Palin as if she were the cover girl for a car magazine and announced: "Conservatives find the girl of their dreams." Despite the misogynistic element in the headline, the article went on to describe Palin's life as the all-American story and credited her with instantly re-energizing the McCain campaign. In true British fashion, another article said that Governor Palin's clothes and glasses made her look like "a naughty librarian."

There is bound to be some condescension in world coverage of the Palin candidacy because the rest of the world long ago began electing powerful women to their highest offices. What can be seen so far is the sharp contrast between McCain's introduction of Palin and the ho-hum response to the news that Joe Biden would be Obama's running mate. The general European media consensus on that selection was "No Threat. But no Asset." The Times' editorialist, William Rees-Mogg, opined that by rejecting Hillary for "a politician with a murky record," Obama might have lost his bid for the White House. Another reporter wondered why Senator Biden was being celebrated more for having lost a wife and child in a car crash than for his voting record and political achievements.

The International Herald Tribune called Palin's entrance into the campaign "pivotal," a "contest recast" that would force both parties to revamp their election year strategies.

The article concluded that the Obama camp would be wise not to run any campaign ads against Palin because they would be sure to backfire. Considering the speed at which an initial negative remark against Governor Palin came flying out of the Obama spin machine, one is tempted to bet this advice will not be heeded.

September 2, 2008

Klaus Against the Greens

For most people, being the president of a country would be enough to keep one busy, but not so for Vaclav Klaus of the Czech Republic. He directs as much time and energy as he possibly can to campaigning against those he characterizes as global warming alarmists. That is why Klaus was delighted when a major Czech daily newspaper ran the complete text of a speech he gave last week -- in Tokyo -- to the The Mont Pelerin Society, a prestigious international economics organizationof which he is a member. Klaus, who has been President of the Czech Republic since 1993, holds a doctorate in economics.

The Tokyo meeting gave President Klaus an opportunity to introduce his new book, "Blue Planet in Green Shackles." The book's subtitle -- What is Endangered: Climate or Freedom? -- reveals Klaus's concern about the totalitarian agenda of environmentalists. He sees no difference between the ideology of communism and that of climate change. He says he is no longer simply concerned about the consequences of politicians using global warming to gain and wield power over ordinary citizens. Klaus describes himself now as "angry." He agrees with author Michael Crichton. "The greatest challenge facing mankind is distinguishing between reality and fantasy, truth from propaganda" as regards global warming.

After he delivered his talk before the MPS, President Klaus sat down for a private interview with HUMAN EVENTS. The man whom Al Gore refused to debate in public when the Czech President challenged him had much to say.

"I am frustrated by the fact that many people, including some leading politicians who privately express similar views to my own, are publicly silent," Klaus began. He believes the global warming issue "is not being debated in a rational way, but is being thrust into the public consciousness as one-sided propaganda." He invokes the term "silent majority" to describe rationally thinking people who do not speak out against global warming propagandists.

Klaus believes that the goal of climate change alarmists is nothing less than a continuation of the socialist model of the centralization of economic control. "They invoke the image of apocalyptic imminent danger in order to trigger the need in others to have a savior -- a messiah," Klaus contends. Then he adds: "The constraints of political correctness are tougher than ever. They are being enforced and only one permitted truth is -- yet again -- imposed on us. Everything else is being denounced."

Klaus contends that global warming has also become "a false identity for the failed United Nations which seeks power over governments and the citizens of the world." Although he concedes that environmentalism evolved from humble and legitimate origins, Klaus calls Al Gore's claim -- that Earth is headed toward "a planetary emergency" -- absurd. He labels it as "scaremongering." "What is being attempted now (by the environmentalist movement) is a form of human behavioral modification, not for purposes of improvement, but for political power."

"Environmentalism has become a quasi-religion," Klaus asserts. "It is an ideology that shares much in common with Marxism. Climate change is the new recruiting strategy for the anti-capitalist, socialist, communist army. They are both monolithic belief systems designed to suppress human freedom." Klaus sees those "who would otherwise reject socialism for what it is -- a system which destroys personal freedom" as being regrettably receptive to global climate change fears. "Propaganda on the false impact of global warming is now being taught by so-called environmentalists to high school students -- just as virtues and correct thinking was taught under communism decades ago."

These are strong words for someone who had to survive under Soviet domination for decades.

"Politicians have been searching for a new topic -- for a very long time -- through which they could control the people because communism and socialism is dead. Global warming is perfect because of escapism. We are far away from the future so that politicians cannot be held responsible for their actions now," Klaus observes.

"When I listened to the G8 meeting in Tokyo a few months ago, each politician proposed ever more ridiculous goals to reduce global warming -- the results of which would not be realized for 100 years. Since the so-called Kyoto global warming treaty was signed, the countries agreed to a reduction of 50% in CO2 goals. Japan's emissions are up 6% -- yet Japan's Prime Minister promised to cut Japan's emissions by 80% in 100 years. Since that meeting just a few months ago, half of those leaders have gone. The Japanese Prime Minister resigned in the first week of September. I am now in Tokyo to meet the head of government. Who should I meet?"

"We will command the wind and the rain! This was an old communist saying well known in the Czech Republic. When I listen to Al Gore, I hear the same objective, except now it's not the wind and the rain they want to control, it's the global environment.

Most people make the mistake of thinking that Mr. Putin is their enemy. They are wrong. Their real enemy -- who would steal their money and personal freedoms -- is Mr. Al Gore."

It is no surprise then that Klaus views global warming quotas and promises by politicians as a means of inflicting untested ideas -- in the form of market controls -- on the international economic engine. This, Klaus says, "gives new life to top down government and controls over people's lives."

"Serious economic consequences are seldom, if ever, discussed," he notes. "Cost benefit studies on plans to reverse global warming are not carried out. Economic theory is discounted." Sadly, he points out, "Less developed countries have been taken hostage by this debate. Environmentalists have placed the growth ability of lesser-developed countries in jeopardy by limiting progress via increasing controls and restrictions. The ultimate victims of green ideology will be the world's poorest people."

"Environmentalism is a movement that intends to change the world radically regardless of the consequences (at the cost of human lives and severe restrictions on individual freedom). It intends to change humankind, human behavior, the structure of society, the system of values -- simply everything," Klaus warns.

President Klaus stresses this point because of his commitment to free market economics. The economist who most influenced his worldview was the late Nobel Prize winner Milton Friedman, whom Klaus regards as the greatest economist of the 20th century. Friedman was one of the original founders of The Mont Pelerin Society.

Klaus describes himself as a short run pessimist, but a long-term optimist. He believes that rationality will trump global warming fundamentalism. He thinks that future generations will look back on this era with amusement and pity for the passion with which this wrong-headed ideology took hold over the minds of primitive 21st century humanity.

In one of his previous books -- which is comprised of speeches given in both Europe and the U.S. between 1996 and 2004 -- Klaus writes, "I came to politics at the age of 48 (after the Velvet Revolution) without thinking about it and without consciously preparing for it." Critics of Sarah Palin, please take note.

September 16, 2008

God vs. Caeser Across the Pond

"Practice What You Preach." It was a headline writer's dream. The Archbishops of Canterbury and York (the two top prelates of the Anglican Communion) were the keynote speakers in London, last week, at the annual dinner of The Worshipful Company of International Bankers (no kidding). They had been asked to address the topic of the world's financial crisis.

The AB of York, John Sentamu, decried an "Alice In Wonderland" market in which the share price of banks were not valued on performance, but on how willing the government might be to buy them out. Sentamu labeled those who profited from selling short "bank robbers" and "asset strippers."

The AB of Canterbury told the bankers that the financial world had become detached from reality and urged governments to be bold in their market interventions.

One single news cycle later, the Church of England stood accused of having used controversial short selling practices in order to maximize profits on its own £5 billion portfolio of investments. A Church spokesperson immediately denied any dubious financial activity, but the books indicate that there was fire where holy smoke had been detected.

The short-selling claim against the COE came from Ekklesia, a British-based religious issues think tank. Jonathan Bartley, co-Director of Ekklesia, called on the COE to "put your money where your mouth is." (Another great headline some wag used). Fellow co-Director, Simon Barrow, observed; "Condemning others while playing the system to your own advantage will strike many as lacking the kind of integrity and creative endeavor the churches could be demonstrating." Barrows is the author of a book entitled, "Is God Bankrupt?" (You can't make this up).

Ekklesia made its claim based on a reading of the 2007 Annual Statement of the Church Commissioners, the group that manages the COE's assets. The document records the COE's holdings in oil and mining companies, banks and properties. The total portfolio averaged a 9.5% return over the past decade -- and it would appear that COE did benefit from speculation in oil, commodities such as gold and copper, and sterling (the British Pound).

Mr. Bartley said the 2007 Report makes no attempt to dissemble the facts. The COE "hedged against a fall in the value of sterling and set up a currency hedging program in 2006, effectively short selling sterling in the currency markets."

Now Jesus did say, Give unto God that which is God's and unto Caesar that which is Caesar's, but this author can find no New Testament verses regarding the morality of taking a profit by betting that your nation's currency is going to tank.

Mr. Bartley's suggestion that the COE should invest in "co-operatives, friendly societies and housing associations which added to the good of the country," was astonishingly ironic in light of the fact that the Archbishop of Canterbury had recently delivered himself of another of his classic epistles. After causing an uproar by advocating for the incorporation of Sharia law into Britain's system of jurisprudence only a few months ago, Rowan Williams took a leap by penning an article on economics and ethics for the conservative magazine The Spectator. His premise was that modern societies had turned wealth into an object of idolatry -- like the proverbial Golden Calf from the time of Moses. Wealth had become the worship of that which you made yourself -- an idol (American or otherwise).

The ABC went on to recognize that entrepreneurs "must be allowed to create wealth to help nations rise out of poverty," but said belief in free market capitalism had now become "a sort of fundamentalism."

"Fundamentalism is a religious word, not inappropriate to the nature of the problem, Williams explained, then added: "Marx long ago observed the way in which unbridled capitalism became a kind of mythology, ascribing reality, power and agency to things that had no life in themselves. He was right about that, if about little else," Williams concluded.

For the record, the Church of England's investments are informed by its own Ethical Investment Advisory Group, over which there appears to be no outside regulator.

Meanwhile, France's President Sarkozy -- now serving as the rotating President of the European Union -- also had something to say about the current financial crisis. Mr. Sarkozy asserted that it was time for capitalism to be reinvented, this time with a strong dose of morality and a sturdy set of regulatory controls. "Laissez faire capitalism is finished," Sarko proclaimed. By this he said he meant that the "all-powerful, under-regulated, marketplace was over and about to be replaced." It was left to the German finance minister, Peer Steinbruck, to coin the term for what comes next: "the multi-polar world."

Steinbruck is a vociferous critic of the US, predicting that its failure to act in preventing this meltdown would result in its loss of its status as a superpower. He told the German Parliament last Thursday: "The world will never be as it was before the crisis." He blamed Washington for blocking stricter regulations, even when it was clear that this crisis was going to roll out last summer.

What Steinbruck seems confused about is which group stood in the way of the reforms which could have stemmed the tide of financial collapses. Steinbruck accused the free market purveyors of laissez faire who maintained an above-all attitude as behind this crisis. The record indicates that there is lots of blame to go around, but it was clearly the Democrats who pressed for affordable housing and blocked all attempts to establish rational regulatory policies to prevent wild-eyed and irresponsible home loans from being handed out to people who – under real free market principles – would not qualify for loans. For clarification have a look at: YouTube - Burning Down The House: What Caused Our Economic Crisis?

Late in the week, UK Prime Minster Gordon Brown flew to Washington to sit next to President Bush for a photo op in the Oval Office. Brown vowed that Britain would back the bailout, adding: "America deserves the support of the rest of the world in securing stability in the markets." Brown had just been up in New York addressing the United Nations where he told the assembly it was time to end "the age of irresponsibility." Say, who has been running the UK government for over a decade?

I'm thinking just the opposite. Perhaps it is time for us to be more responsible by tossing a few greedy CEO's and self-interested bureaucrats into Boston Harbor as if they were tea.

If Bill Clinton had good intentions when he sent Janet Reno out to force banks to begin granting sub prime mortgages (or else), then he has proven that old axiom about what paves (or in this case 'redlines') the road to hell. And when the Archbishop of Canterbury short sells sterling and finds a silver lining in Marxism, there would seem to be fellow travelers going down the road with us.

September 30, 2008

United in Uncharted Territory

It is nearing midnight in Paris as this copy is being written. A joint press release has just been issued following an emergency meeting on Sunday between the leaders of the 15 Eurozone (single currency) nations and UK Prime Minister Gordon Brown. Acting EU and French President Nicholas Sarkozy said he expected one and all to act in unison.

"The crisis has over the past few days entered into a phase that makes it intolerable to opt for procrastination and a go-it-alone approach," he said.

A round of talks will be held in Brussels on Wednesday, but last night the bankers were still at work -- literally burning the midnight oil. By all accounts, Europe and England now seem to be marching in lock step toward the creation of partly nationalized banking systems.

Sarkozy announced that all parties had agreed; "no big institution would be allowed to fail." Loans between banks would be guaranteed until the end of 2009, with governments putting the capital in by purchasing preference shares. Greedy financiers would be prevented from finding ways of benefiting from this intervention. Managers to whom blame could be assigned would be dismissed from their positions. The French love gilt and military displays, but Sarkozy made it clear that there would be no more golden parachutes. Non.

But it remains to be seen if this plan will prevent continuing panic in the world's markets.

Britain introduced a similar rescue plan last week. Over the weekend, an influential Sunni Muslim cleric took pleasure in claiming this crisis proves Islamic economics are superior to capitalism. Usury -- charging excessive or unbridled interest on loans -- is not permitted under Islamic law. And Allah apparently frowns on sub-prime mortgages. The cleric's gloat was underscored by a rather macabre news item. British funeral directors were out complaining to the press that dead bodies were starting to pile up because the government was "dragging its feet" in sending out checks to cover burial expenses for poor families. The government claimed that checks were going out in 16 days "on average." The statistics here are staggering. 27,000 people claim a total of £46 million for burials every year in Britain. This apparently includes handling and transport fees, a coffin, and up to £700 for a vicar to give the send-off. There's fiduciary responsibility for you!

As for the retired and elderly, one financial specialist speculated that £150 billion has been wiped off the value of British pensions in the past year alone. John Maples, a deputy chairman of the Conservative (Tory) Party, said that half a dozen chairmen and chief executives from among major British banks should do the "honourable thing" and leave their jobs.

It seems neither comforting nor convincing that the British bureaucracy -- already so bogged down in paperwork and inefficiency -- can now suddenly rise to meet the unprecedented economic challenges it faces. By the way, the Tories have demanded an emergency Commons debate on the funeral problem. Talk about ghoulish reality TV.

European Commission President Jose Manuel Barroso expressed his hope that the EU plan would end "the excessive pessimism of the markets." But other experts are not persuaded that this worldwide meltdown can be halted in time to prevent a continuing cascade, which will hurt the poor in developing nations. World Bank President Robert Zoellick asserted the most vulnerable nations could still sustain "serious -- and in some cases permanent -- damage."

His fears were supported by what happened to the highly sophisticated, albeit tiny, nation of Iceland. Far from being a developing nation, Iceland was seen as a model of modernity and enterprise. But when its banking system all but failed last week, the British went ballistic. It emerged that small British investors and some local British authorities and charities had invested billions of pounds in one particular Icelandic bank.

For a few days, the two island nations teetered on a near war-like footing until a financial détente -- a promise to make these losses whole -- was achieved through diplomatic efforts. Who could have imagined Iceland and England at each other's throats? Or that Russia (determined to re-create a new world empire) would offer to bail out Iceland's banks? We are truly in uncharted -- and very dangerous -- territory.

More gloating was heard from those who had it in for Maggie Thatcher. They pointed out that her government had let the dogs of deregulation loose in "The City" (as the financial square mile in London is known). To socialists and unionists, seeing any portion of the UK renationalized is sweet justice. The Royal family has remained utterly silent. So much for British fireside chats.

Just a week ago, the Prime Minister of France, Francois Fillon, looking decidedly glum and existential, lamented that the world was now on the edge of an abyss. The Sunday Times' headline carried a dire warning from Dominque Strauss-Kahn, President of the International Monetary Fund. He predicted that world markets could still collapse by another 20 percent before things were stabilized.

BBC TV reporters took a knock for not keeping a stiff upper lip. Their brethren in the print media chastised them for rushing out with stories of disaster and default at the top of every news cycle.

Market reactions and the Brussels meeting on Wednesday will provide the next chapters in this unbelievable saga.

October 14, 2008

Obama Kept Talks with Gene Robinson Quiet During Campaign

Who among us will ever forget those audio tapes of the Rev. Jeremiah Wright damning America from his Chicago pulpit and the impression that the Obamas sat in that congregation for years, affirming this stridency with their "Amens"?

We also all know that once the Wright tapes -- and his speech at the National Press Club -- proved to be politically wrong, candidate Obama had an epiphany and -- as if he was hearing the higher authority from Mission Impossible headquarters in his brain -- knew he had to deny any knowledge of the Wright operation.

Newsweek did a cover article on Obama entitled "Finding His Faith" and revealed the President-elect to be a self-styled spiritual seeker. He was exposed to many faith traditions before deciding to be baptized as a Christian when he was an adult.

So what's up now -- theologically -- with our President Elect? Granted, he's been too busy to go to church during the campaign and has said he will not attend one while in office. As Ronald Reagan had discerned during his Presidency, it is unfair to the members of any congregation to have their worship services subject to the untender mercies of Secret Service protection and the inevitable press invasions. Can't fault him for that.

But there are some behind-the-scenes Obama religious encounters that have received very little U.S. media attention. Once again, the Times of London scooped the lethargic American media. The most unusual of these encounters requires a preface in the form of a breaking domestic religious news item.

Last week, the Diocese of Fort Worth, Texas, became the

fourth such entity to break with the U.S. Episcopal Church hierarchy, choosing to align itself with a traditionalist South American province. The vote to secede -- which passed by a wide majority -- is part of an on-going denominational dispute that began with the 2003 consecration of Gene Robinson, an openly gay Bishop. To refer to the New Hampshire Bishop as a controversial figure in the religious world is an understatement.

Not once, or twice, but three times it emerges -- during May and June -- candidate Obama and the Bishop had private talks. Robinson broke the story during an interview with The Times. He was in London to receive the "Hero of the Year" award from the gay rights organization, Stonewall. According to Robinson, the first thing Sen. Obama said to him was: "Well, you're certainly causing a lot of trouble," to which the Bishop replied: "Well, that makes two of us."

Robinson described the entire series of encounters with Obama as "a religious experience," (clever). They reportedly talked about "what it was like to be first," about how to handle being demonized by one's opponents, and the place of religion in state affairs.

Robinson claims that these conversations are illustrative of Obama's extraordinary outreach to all religious communities, not just Christian groups. Candidates for office are, of course, entitled to seek out advice from anyone they chose, but it is curious that the Obama campaign kept this trio of chats under wraps. When the news spreads, it will certainly add fuel to the Episcopal fire that has brought that church to the brink of a schism.

It can also be construed as an insult to the members of the Worldwide Anglican Communion in Africa. The Bishops of Africa find great difficulty in being part of a church that supports gay rights. They are competing for members against Islam, which regards homosexuality as a sin punishable by death. The cultural bias in African countries favors the Muslim position on gender issues. By seeking out an openly gay clergyman for private counsel, Obama risks alienating both Christians and Muslims in Africa.

There are no reports that the President-elect sought out any Catholic clergy during his campaign. He, did, however, receive a phone call from Pope Benedict after the election. That courtesy call came on the same day in which the Vatican also warned Obama not to lift the current U.S. ban on stem cell research, which he has promised to do. The Vice President-elect, Joe Biden, is already in hot water with the Catholic Church for misrepresenting Church teachings on abortion. Ditto Speaker of the House Nancy Pelosi. But election demographics indicate that Catholics no longer vote according to doctrine but according to their stances on social issues.

Which brings us -- finally -- to the lost tribe of Barack Obama, a family tale with religious and political overtones. Once again, it was The Times of London which reported this intriguing story. It all began when a 95-year-old woman in the Bedouin community of Bir al-Maksour -- located in the very Biblical area of Galilee -- noticed a family resemblance between Obama and some of the women in the tribe. This group of Bedouins was once a semi-nomadic group with roots in Syria. Many are converts to Islam.

Abdul Rahman Sheikh Abdullah, a local council member, saw the resemblance too. It seems that African migrant workers used to be employed by the rich sheikhs who resided just north of the British Mandate of Palestine in the 1930s. The Africans often married local Bedouin girls and one of those migrant men was apparently a relative of Obama's Kenyan grandmother (who is still alive). The tribe of 8000 kept quiet about their possible family ties to candidate Obama, not wishing to inject this element into the American electoral process. Word of Obama's connection to the tribe has caused great excitement in the Arab community in Northern Israel. A party is being planned. The question -- yet to be addressed -- is how Obama's family ties could affect U.S. foreign policy in the already muddled Middle East situation.

November 19, 2008

Europe is on Suicide Watch

For the past few days, more than two million Muslims from around the world have been participating in the Hajj. This time around, it has been peaceful. No deaths reported.

The Hajj is a religious obligation required of all able-bodied Muslims at least once in their lives. The Kingdom of Saudi Arabia maintains a Ministry of Hajj website which requests all pilgrims to "Be peaceful, orderly and kind. No crushing." But the world's population of Muslims has grown to the point where hundreds of them have been regularly trampled to death during this annual demonstration of submission to Allah. The crushing occurs as masses of pilgrims circle -- seven times -- around the Kaaba, a large black stone in the center of the shrine's walled courtyard. Kissing the stone was dropped as a part of the process a while back when it became clear that Mecca had a traffic flow problem. A set of "confidential" plans were drawn up and funded, allegedly by Saudi King Abdullah bin Abdul Aziz. Seems this time they listened, but a better day lies ahead.

Back in Europe, two of Britain's most popular and award-winning architects have been chosen to work with a group of select peers, engineers and construction specialists, on a multi-billion dollar redevelopment project. The mission in this case is to remodel Mecca itself. It seems Islam's holiest shrine, and the city surrounding it, are in need of an extreme makeover to better accommodate the millions of pilgrims who participate in the Hajj.

The master vision includes building a mosque that can hold three million people. Plans for the metropolis known as Modern Mecca, where the pilgrims once searched for limited accommodations, call for flattening all nearby homes and hills and filling in the reclaimed real estate with 130 skyscrapers. No word yet on how many additional Starbucks franchise operations will join the pioneer branches already in operation in the holy city.

Meanwhile, in Rome, Magdi Cristiano Allam has launched a new program. He is the Egyptian-born writer who -- after converting from Islam to Christianity -- was baptized last Easter by Pope Benedict XVI in the Vatican. Already under armed guard because he is continually receiving threats to his life (apostasy from Islam is punishable by death) from his former Muslim brethren, Allam (who became an Italian citizen in 1986) raised more hackles this week when he announced his latest project. He is forming a new political party called "Protagonists for a Christian Europe," which hopes to field candidates in European parliamentary elections next June.

The Protagonist Party's standard combines a circle of 12 stars superimposed on the Italian national flag. The banner bears the words "Truth and Liberty," "Faith and Reason," and "Values and Rules." Mr. Allam believes that someone needs to defend Europe's Christian values, which are threatened by secularism and moral relativism. In a nutshell, the Party's manifesto is to "stop Europe from committing suicide." This will take a great deal of intervention.

The Europeans continue to make news in unusual ways.

The Swiss just voted to issue heroin on a prescription basis, while turning down an initiative to decriminalize cannabis. As Roger Boyes observed, in a Times editorial, "it is clear that the Swiss do more than cuckoo clocks." He tried to envision Heidi legally shooting up.

The Greeks have fire bombed their government-erected Christmas tree and are engaged in ongoing rioting throughout the country. The Romanians (new members of the EU) have just elected an essentially Communist parliament. Back to the future?

For comic relief, France has recently endured the usual litany of strikes. Pilots, teachers, transportation employees, and a post office staff all conducted protests, but President Sarkozy had a hard time keeping his eye on those balls. He was engaged in a lawsuit to have production of a voodoo doll, made in his image, to be immediately stopped. He lost the case -- much to the delight of the beleaguered Socialist Party. The appeals judge affirmed that "spearing the doll according to the instructions and with the provided needles -- an action that evokes physical albeit symbolic harm -- constitutes an offense to the dignity of Mr. Sarkozy," but he did not ban its manufacture. Instead, the judge instructed the company, which makes the dolls to add a warning labels to its boxes, which state that, the doll, is "an offense to the dignity of the President." Sarko's detractor's say he has finally found his "inner De Gaulle."

And then we come full circle.

A recent study indicates that the British have become "much lonelier" over the past 30 years. This conclusion emerged from the serious research of a collection of academics who set out to identify the most isolated places in the UK, defining those as places where people "were most likely to experience feelings of not belonging." Belonging to what, one wonders? Last week a teenage boy committed suicide, allegedly because his Christianity was being crushed by political correctness.

Perhaps not unrelated is a scientific study which found that the attention span of the average Briton is now reckoned to be down to an average of five minutes. The UK's national case of attention deficit disorder obviously accounts for the alarm raised by the Lloyds TBS Insurance Company financial summary for 2007. Lloyd's expressed concern about the number of incidents that could be directly traced to things like fires from forgotten pans on stove tops and bathtubs which overflowed.

Covering the damage claims these incidents engendered cost UK insurance companies a whopping one-year total of $2.5 billion. Astonishingly, the Lloyd's report concluded that these incidents were "due to people not concentrating properly." Toss in UK stats on binge drinking, drug abuse, anorexia, anti-social crimes, and general apathy. A clinical diagnosis of a country prone to suicide seems hard to refute.

But if the average Briton is searching for community and something that focuses one's attention, they ought to avert their eyes from the ever-trendy Church of England. It has just printed comic books called "Christmas Crackers" as part of an online seasonal holiday teaching project. "Christmas Crackers" comics (named for trinket-filled favors one pops apart before eating Christmas dinner) are designed to make the holiday season "fresh and relevant" to the children in the Church of England's 479 parishes and 130 schools, and accessible on the Diocese's dedicated Christmas website www.londonchristmas.org.uk.

In the pages of the Crackers, children are treated to images of the Holy Family with captions that explain the good news. Mary is the Mum, and she's got a husband, but (surprise) "God's the Dad." The sociological implications are staggering.

There are also images of Santa and snowmen. Clearly missed by the authors of the gospel nativity narratives, it now appears that Santa and snowmen were sitting around the Bethlehem hillsides with the shepherds who were guarding their flocks by night. One supposes Santa's reindeer were grazing nearby and that Rudolph's red nose led the lot of them to the stable. Oh Holy.... Night....

Yes indeed, the EU's new Protagonist Party has its work cut out for it.

December 11, 2008

No Political Good Will for Christmas in England

If the Labour Party, currently headed by Prime Minister Gordon Brown, thought it had been politically nice during its past decade plus in power, five of the most senior gentleman Anglican Bishops in England just laid that ungodly idea to rest.

Three days after Christmas, in an historically unprecedented - decidedly non-goodwill - gesture, the five dismayed Bishops (each in separate but precisely synchronized statements delivered to The Telegraph newspaper) declared that the Labour Party had not only been naughty, it had been found guilty of transplanting a moral vacuum where the heart of the United Kingdom once beat. Casting themselves in the role of post-modern wise men, (or perhaps the ghosts of Christmas Present) were the Bishops from Carlisle, Durham, Hulme, Manchester, and Winchester respectively.

The Bishop of Manchester accused Labour of being "beguiled by money." The Bishop of Hulme said Labour was "morally suspect." The Bishop of Winchester (yes, there is a Winchester Cathedral a dodeodoe) and the Bishop of Carlisle claimed that Labour had "squandered their opportunity to transform society and had run out of steam." Tom Wright of Durham said the government had not done enough to help the poor.

These were not tidings of comfort and joy to Labour MPs (Members of Parliament) and the statements evoked some less than seasonal greetings from the halls of government. One crotchety MP suggested the Bishops had been imbibing too much traditional holiday mulled wine. Likewise, Prime Minster Brown was said to be furious rather than full of Christmas cheer.

The citizens of the earthly kingdom were asked to contemplate: Was this current catastrophe a sign that they were to return to an Upstairs Downstairs scenario? Or was this to be the next Great Depression -- or worse -- The Age of Dickens Redux?

The Bishops blamed the financial magi for keeping the gifts of gold for themselves, using the incense for the smoke value, while the humble folk had been enticed into a flock of debt and were now left sheepishly bankrupt. Alas, that image does not wash. Years ago, when he was the head of the Treasury under Tony Blair, Gordon Brown sold off most of the nation's gold when it had all but bottomed out in price. Billions disappeared then, too.

So now it had all come down to One Holy financial Nightmare, lamented the five Bishops. Rather than heralding a new age of socially redeeming consciousness and public services, the Bishops characterized Labour as the new Herod & Co. The Party was nothing more than a self-serving lot which had reneged on its promises. This had resulted in a nation of broken families (the slaying of the first born to be substituted by abortions) and a burgeoning divide between the rich and the poor. The system had been distorted, the wise Five wailed. It was all the fault of politicians, they sang in chorus.

Yes, as if they were a single voice from on high, the Bishops said that "Nu Labour" had sacrificed the principles of Old Labour (take from the rich and give to the poor and do whatever the Unions ask of you) for the sake of votes. While promising a humanitarian future, Nu Labour had delivered, instead of aspirations, a message of hopelessness. Money and jobs had or were vanishing. Pensions funds had disappeared. The National Health Service was as screwed up as ever, and yet the tabloids continued to lift up the exploits of the rich and famous as if nothing had or ever could touch them. Every one was watching reality TV despite a warning from the ever-amusing Archbishop of Canterbury (the week before Christmas) that we should not wait for a super hero to save us. Yeah verily. Some dared to think he was talking about Obama.... And others wondered if he was referring to the Christ child...

But as one editorialist exclaimed: " Nobody apart from a handful of deranged free-marketeers - who yearn for a return to the brutality of the Victorian era -- are opposed to state benefits." The December 30th issue of the Daily Mail (for example) exclaimed: "The welfare system is testimony to our caring society, but politicians have turned it into a monster that is slowly destroying Britain." This referred to the most recent government figures indicating that 140,000 households were drawing down £20,000 a year (or more) in "handouts," a sum which is more than the take-home pay of many average workers.

Half of all working women in the UK earn less than £21,424 a year and one in ten full time employees lives on less than £13,613 before tax. Prisoners are receiving cash payments along with early releases from jail. A family of seven was just found to be living in a £2.6 million (government subsidized) house in a ritzy part of town at taxpayer expense. FYI – all state benefits are tax free. Tracing back the historical record belies the charges of latter day piracy and corruption. All roads seem to lead to a gradual transition from the creation of a social safety net to a system known here as "the dole," a network of government programs which are like drugs. They get people hooked on freebies and then wonder at the rising cost of these addictions to the productive members of society. Those who can create jobs and lift all the boats are left feeling like enablers.

Enter the religious factor. There is a growing movement afoot to disestablish the Church of England from the monarchy and the government structure over which the Queen very loosely reigns. The Bishops who decry the disintegration of family units are also the first to be found on the front lines of the fight for multi-cultural sensitivity and a blanket theology of situational ethics which makes a hash of the Christian principles they are supposed to represent.

All the preaching these five Bishops have done appears to be less like angelic hosts serving up the good news and more of an academic committee revisiting the same old economic and theological punchbowl. The cup which no longeth runneth over – as they see it – serves to prove the incompatibility of Christianity and capitalism. The twist of modernity in this recipe is that the Big UK Five have spiked their temporal brew with a smidgeon of Gordon Gecko and called it Brown.

The sorry part is that David Cameron, leader of the conservative (Tory) Party, played into the Bishops' hands. He chimed in with the Bishops, proclaiming that England's current precarious position – poised as it is on the verge of bankruptcy - was going to become the political epitaph of Gordon Brown. He did not deflect any of the explicit or implicit attacks on Margaret Thatcher's policies (which are becoming reflex ammo lobbed adhoc by the left), nor did he say anything particularly bold (except a mild promise to lower some taxes). Worse, by the end of the week he was alluding to Gaza and accused Gordon Brown of lobbing bombs on the economy. The man is obviously a member of the Metaphor of the week club. This does not bode well for a man who might find himself trying to lead the United Kingdom out of one of the most troubled times in its history. Where are the REAL wise men. Or women?

Postscript: The December 31st edition of the Evening Standard carries a bold type headline quote from Boris Johnson, London's slightly wacky somewhat conservative Mayor. It reads: 2009 Could Be A Year of Hope. To paraphrase the President-elect, "Yes, it could."

December 31, 2008

The Church of England Invests in Al Gore

Pravda means Truth in Russian and -- on Sunday the 11th of January -- Matt Drudge ran a Pravda story in which the old Soviet -- now "free press" -- outlet proclaimed that "Earth is on the brink of an ice age." It must be true, by definition.

This headline followed a week of interesting weather news in Europe. The fountain in London's Trafalgar Square froze over, as did Bembridge Harbor off the Isle of Wight. Thursday the 8th of January was the coldest day in Britain for seven years. The head of the state owned energy supplier in France warned of power shortages if the cold snapcontinued. Russia chose this frigid week to turn down the natural gas pipeline to Eastern Europe.

The cold weather was blamed for six deaths in Poland and Germany. In the Netherlands, government ministries and multinational firms gave employees a day off last Thursday so they could all go skating across that nation's frozen canals and lakes. An estimated 2.3 million people did just that. In northern Italy, motorways were closed after 60 hours of incessant snowfalls. Snow fell on the palm trees in Marseille, the southern most French Mediterranean port. Further south, a freak snowstorm shut down Madrid's airport and so on and so on. In a nutshell, evidence of the ice age was omnipresent.

All of this came to pass during the first week of January when Vaclav Klaus, President of the Czech Republic -- and highly visible global warming skeptic -- took over the rotating Presidency of The European Union for his six month term. News doesn't get any more ironic than this.... Or does it?

Well it does if you are reading about the investment portfolio of the Commissioners of The Church of England. Last September, this 33 member aggregate body - made up of notable COE clergy and assorted esteemed lay people - voted to place £150 million (or $225 million) into the hands of Generation Investment Management.

GIM is the "boutique management" firm founded by Al Gore and run by his managing partner, David Blood. This pairing is widely known in the financial world as "Blood and Gore." The GIM entity has also now been christened "The Carbon Empire," a painful blow to those who remember the old British Empire where -- over the weekend -- the government backed an EU policy suggestion that plasma TVs should be banned because they are energy hogs.

Meanwhile, as in the US, those damnable "energy saving" compact fluorescent light bulbs are now being forced into people's homes in the United Kingdom, despite irrefutable evidence that the amount of mercury these bulbs contain requires a hazmat clean-up if broken. They also can cause seizures and migranes. Curiously, a former Labour Party minister, Lord (Joel) Barnett, now known as Lord Light Bulb, now finds himself in a bright entrepreneurial spot. In the mid 1990's, he created a company that specializes in toxic mercury bulb handling.

The Mercury Recycling Group already holds exclusive and lucrative contracts with schools and local authorities and literally stands to clean up when all incandescent bulbs are completely phased out by 2011. The Environment Department is instructing individuals to carefully take their burned out bulbs to -- what else -- government approved operations, most of which will be run by Mercury Recycling. Lord Light Bulb's company also could be looking at governme nt funded bounties if its employees snitch on citizens with outlawed plasma screens in their sitting rooms.

Now, if you are still suffering from an irony deficiency, here's a supplement. Turns out these toxic low-energy bulbs are incompatible with half of all lamps and fixture sockets in British homes. Nor do they work with dimmer controls. This news -- presented in a report by The Department of Environment, Food, and Rural Affairs -- prompted millions of consumers to brave last week's freezing temperatures in order to empty the stocks of traditional bulbs from the shelves of several major retailers. Even so, their choices were limited. 150-watt bulbs were withdrawn from sale in Britain last year. The 60 watter will be banned beginning in 2010.

This suggests that while the UK economy endures a recession, the populace faces either sitting in the dark, or in very bright fluorescently lit rooms, watching old black and white tellies they had kept for their potential value as collectible antiques if the road show ever came to their towns. Sales of Gin and Tonic are bound to soar under these conditions.

In the days leading up to Christmas, five Anglican Bishops accused the Labour government of being morally corrupt and insensitive to the poor, but they seem to have said nothing, on the record, as regards the Church of England's significant investment in what has been called Al Gore's massive Ponzi Scheme. The Church Commissioners might have done themselves a service by reading the August 2008 and August 2007 issues of the Capital Research Center's (www.capitalresearch.org) publication, Foundation Watch. Both take Al Gore to the proverbial woodshed, assessing his activities as means to benefit his own ends first and foremost.

The bottom line for GIM investors depends on politicians continuing to legislate insane policies on the pretext of keeping everything green. That will insure that Blood and Gore will see the green keep rolling into their corporate accounts from the woefully misinformed and foolish.

Several questions come to mind. Does The Church of England risk going bankrupt if Pravda is right about the new Ice Age? Will people stop going to church entirely if there is no heat? Cold hard pews are hard to fill. Does all of this portend a new cliché? What happens when Heaven freezes over?

January 14, 2008

Le Inauguration

They were the hottest tickets in town. Bertrand Delanoe, Mayor of Paris, had invited about 1700 American expats to view the "retransmission of the ceremony of investiture" of the 44th President of the United States, "Son Excellence Monsieur Barack Obama," in the ornate Hotel de Ville (City Hall).

In the spirit of fairness, Delanoe had arranged for the invitations to be distributed equally between liberals and conservatives. The liberal tickets were gone in a heartbeat, but there were only a few conservatives on hand. The gentleman who was given charge of the conservative tickets had, earlier in the week, come under fire when their existence became known to a few frustrated Democrats, and he refused to hand over the precious invitations. A man of principle.

There was a line on the street which doubled back on itself leading up to a side entrance. As soon as one came through the rather casual security checkpoint, the red carpet began, leading one into the entrance of this grand monument to French architecture which sits in distinguished fashion on the banks of the River Seine. Impressive paintings line the walls and majestic statues stand in hallways and along the wide center-staircase. In the main reception rooms, chandeliers, glistening like diamonds, were hung from lavishly embellished ceilings.

Large screens had been set up in several rooms. By 5 p.m. Paris time, CNN's coverage was well underway, and the crowd's excitement was palpable. When a CNN camera caught Vice President Dick Cheney being wheeled into the Capitol, the first of many heartfelt "boos" swelled among the ranks. In the main hall, the mayor, associate mayor, and the U.S. Ambassador to France had taken their places up on a podium. French television news crews weaved in and out of the standing audience, often nearly colliding with one another in their attempts to interview any and all interested parties.

At one point, the giant screens went dark and the mayor introduced the Golden Gate Quartet, four African American gentlemen who belted out a very jazzy version of America's National Anthem. They began singing it a second time, much more reverentially and invited the audience to sing along. Many did. A few placed their hands over their hearts. Several guests had thought to bring American flags.

These were the same people who, back in April, cheered candidate Obama when he visited France. They were also active in fund raising and making sure that the turnout of American voters in Paris -- and in other regions - was record-breaking.

The mayor took back the microphone and made a little speech, then handed it over to the U.S. ambassador, who did likewise. But by this time, the crowd was getting restless. A few people started chanting CNN, and they were quickly joined by the rest of the audience. Not wishing to start an insurrection, the screens were turned back on without further delay.

Paris was awash with images of Obama last week. His face was on virtually every daily newspaper, both French and international. Le Figaro put a stylish photo of Obama on the cover of its Sunday magazine. There were special inserts with coverage of the week's events and stirring editorials on the "nouveau America" which was about to be realized. But Obama's image was also being used in more commercial ways. Subway posters -- designed to sell a set of new encyclopedias -- featured the face of George Washington wearing an Obama '08 baseball cap. And on the Champs Elysees, the Virgin Record Store had put up a large image of Obama with Mount Rushmore as the backdrop -- as if he was sure to be up there some day. How many denizens of Paris understood the iconic visual message is not reported.

As the time for the actual "investiture" neared, the guests in City Hall were getting more anxious. When it became clear that the proceedings were running late, Wolf Blitzer's voice could be heard explaining that Obama had legally become President at high noon, with or without the oath. A cheer went up and people began talking among themselves up to the moment when the swearing in began.

When President Obama began his speech, a reverential hush descended. The assembled crowd undoubtedly expected a barn-burning, side-winding declaration of a new age. There was a phrase in which Obama spoke of Christians and Muslims, Jews and Hindus, and people of no faith. To that latter category -- of no faith -- applause broke out around the room. So much for the religious left. An article in the French magazine devoted to religion mentioned that Obama's parents were essentially secular and his brand of Christianity was his own, albeit grounded in tradition. The Inauguration Day edition of the left leaning newspaper Liberation had depicted Obama's face in a prayer-like pose, describing him as having "profound sincerity" and referring to the huge promise he was bringing to the world.

One French pundit observed that only American politicians ended speeches with the invocation of "God bless America." This was, he explained, because Americans believe in their country's manifest destiny as a national religion. No confusion over separation of church and state in this scenario, one is bound to notice.

The more militaristic elements of Obama's speech seemed to generate a similar confusion among the assembled liberals. There were no other noticeable breakouts of applause and, when it ended, there were no cheers to match the very vocal boos aimed at Bush and Cheney earlier. The next noise to capture one's attention were the popping of champagne corks -- and it was the good stuff. Perrier Jouet. People moved from room to room, or looked out of the windows at the Seine, perhaps trying to see some sign of the new world they felt had begun.

There was but one last communal moment to the evening's festivities. Although Obama had said that it was time to put away childish things, the crowds all waved when the helicopter carrying Mr. and Mrs. Bush departed Washington, D.C. From around the room, there were various shouts. "Good riddance," goodbye," "enjoy your exile in Texas." Then it was back to the champagne and gourmet hors'd oeuvres and dreams of how "le premiere President noir" would transform the world.

January 29, 2009

The Pope Screws Up -- Again

Pope Benedict XVI's defenders claim that he meant well, but he seems to have a talent for proving that no good deed goes unpunished. Like President Obama's recent cabinet kerfuffles, this incident is surely another example of what happens when you don't vet people properly. It also illustrates that issuing a hasty policy decision can backfire. Here is the twisted tale.

In late January, Pope Benedict overturned a 1988 decision made by John Paul II lifting the bans of excommunication pronounced against four Bishops who were -- and continue to be -- followers of a (deceased) break-away French-born Archbishop named Marcel Lefebrve. Among the restored quartet was Archbishop Richard Williamson, an Englishman serving as the head of a seminary in Argentina.

Excommunication, for those not familiar with theological terminology, is the most serious censure the Catholic Church can impart. It means one has been found guilty of a grave offense, punishable by exclusion from the communion and community of the church. Not a final judgment, an excommunication can be overturned if the person is deemed to have returned to "the path of righteousness." It is worth noting that, prior to becoming pope, Cardinal Joseph Ratzinger was the Head of the Congregation for the Doctrine of the Faith at the Vatican. This office evolved from its early roots, when it was known as the Inquisition. No one knows heretics like Ratzinger, which makes this story all the more unbelievable.

Let's begin with the question of why Lefebrve and his followers were excommunicated.

Lefebrve was not in favor of the modernizing changes made during the Second Vatican Council in the 1960's (i.e. no more services in Latin, turning around the altars and such). His frustration mounted until, in 1970, he founded the Society of St. Pius X (the SSPX). Approached by seminarians who shared his feelings that the church had lost its way, Lefebrve began trying to create a seminary for these traditionalists. The project began well, but dogmatic clashes broke out and final recognition was denied for both the school and priestly order. Lefebrve appealed. He went to the Vatican to make his case and the discussions reportedly became hostile. In the end, the SSPX was ordered to dissolve itself. It did not. Lefebrve defied the Vatican and was excommunicated. Among other things, this meant he was no longer supposed to ordain priests, but he ignored that ban as well. Some hard core conspiratorialists assert that Lefebrve's own ordination was not valid because the French Cardinal who performed that service was actually a Freemason -- grounds for excommunication from the Catholic Church since 1884. But I digress.

Fast forward to 2009 when -- ostensibly to bring the several hundred SSPX members back into the fold -- Benedict reversed his predecessor's decree against the "illegally" ordained renegades. Richard Williamson was among those whom Lefebrve consecrated both as a priest and, years later, as a Bishop.

The problem was that, just a few days earlier, during an interview on Swedish television, Williamson discussed his view that the history of the Holocaust had been grossly exaggerated. He stated that only a few hundred thousand Jews - not six million - had been killed by the Nazis in concentration camps. Rather than exhibiting righteousness, Williamson's remarks unleashed a firestorm many have since compared to the bombing of Dresden in World War Two. How could a pope -- from Germany of all places -- reignite a debate about the Holocaust and besmirch his own papacy in the bargain? The Vatican's level of participation in the Holocaust (active or passive) and its role in helping to relocate Nazi war criminals is the subject of dozens of books and of on-going lawsuits for claims against the Vatican bank. Perhaps coincidently, the highest legal authority in France just acknowledged that the country had failed to save imperiled Jews during WW2.

Incredulity and anger about Williamson's "rehabilitation" erupted in all quarters. Angela Merkel, Chancellor of Germany, entered the fray, saying Benedict was an embarrassment to his country. This prompted an unprecedented and spirited defense from Benedict's brother. A prominent German theologian called for the pope to retire. An editorial in the influential German publication -- der Spiegel -- said the Williamson affair had done lasting damage to Benedict's reputation and to the authority of the Church. To underscore the idea that Benedict was out of touch, der Spiegel ran a photo of a solitary Benedict waving from a window in his papal jet.

Benedict's initial response to this uproar was to issue an official statement indicating he had not known of Williamson's views. Later, when it became clear that the clamor was not dying down, the Pope declared that Williamson would have to recant his remarks, not least of all because being a Holocaust denier is a criminal offense in Germany. Like Lefebrvre before him, Williamson did no such thing and a few days later, the Bishop was fired from his post as head of the seminary in Argentina.

During that week, the Vatican's press department was spinning as fast as it could. They explained that this pope had halved the press/communications office budget and staff time. It was sheer irony that this "excuse" was being put out in the same week that the Pope got his own YouTube Channel so he could "engage with people where ever they are."

Vatican insiders were livid over this latest public relations debacle, recalling what had happened a few years back when a sentence, in a speech delivered by Benedict, caused a violent backlash by Muslims. Media outlets observed that the Williamson incident had exposed "fissures" within the Vatican hierarchy. This was an understatement.

Vatican sources confided to the press that this pope listened only to a handful of advisors -- a tiny cadre who did not represent the geographical diversity of the Curia. And because Benedict had become so insular, he was increasingly prone to playing his role on the world stage with a tin ear. This time, he seemed to have jeopardized years of conciliatory dialogue with the Jewish community. Again, the press office issued an overnight statement which declared that the Vatican's dialogue with the Jews remained "fluid," but behind-the-scenes some extreme measures were being taken.

By the middle of last week, a private meeting with Benedict had been organized. Attending were prominent members of a variety of Jewish organizations and leaders of the faith. Those who were party to this gathering reported that Benedict said all the things you would expect and was aware that he had made a mistake.

This brought another interesting issue to the fore. In the late 19th century, the Catholic Church invented the doctrine of papal infallibility. According to this policy, nothing a pope says on matters of faith can be challenged. Curiously, the Williamson incident had elicited a sort of "mea culpa" from a sitting pope. What happens to the idea of infallibility when the pope has faith in his advisors and they fail him?

It is still early days to assess how badly this whole episode has hurt Benedict – indeed even how it has damaged the papacy. After his meeting with Jewish representatives, the Vatican announced that the pope's visit to the Holy Land would happen on schedule.

It is suspicious that (Catholic) Nancy Pelosi insisted the Senate vote on the stimulus package so quickly because she had to fly to Rome for a week. Nancy is not on the pope's good side right now after misrepresenting Catholic teachings on "Meet the Press." Maybe she's hoping for a quick dispensation while Benedict is preoccupied with the fallout from the Bishop Williamson affair.

February 18, 2009

Cooler Heads May Prevail in Climate Debate

If you are a religious zealot when it comes to global warming and a devoted follower of the movement's high priest, Al Gore, please skip this article. We already know we nonbelievers are going to burn here on earth before we eventually burn in hell. Don't bother posting some rant. We've heard it all before. Thanks.

If, however, you are rational and open to the results of scientific research, please proceed.

A new level of activism among climate realists emerged during the second week in March in New York City when The Heartland Institute hosted its second annual International Conference on Climate Change. It is rare that a conference transcends its format, its brilliant assembly of experts and participants, and becomes something greater than the whole. This was one of those events, where a new society of U.S.- based scientists was born: professors, economists, government experts, journalists and elected officials, who are committed to pursuing the truth in climate science. Launched out of an existing scientific organization in Canada (The International Climate Science Center based in Ottawa), this new entity will allow this prestigious group of scientists -- as they have chosen to rebrand themselves -- to coalesce their energies and become a coordinated chorus, one which the global warming alarmists of the world have tried to silence on an individual basis.

The Heartland Institute's Journalist's Guide to Global Warming Experts can assist any objective media person who seeks relevant scholarly opinions which contradict those held by the alarmists.

Be aware: The guest speakers and contributing panelists from 14 nations, and many of the attendees who came from 24 nations, did not have an easy journey on the way to this conference.

For taking a stand against global warming alarmism, they have been slandered in the halls of academia, denied grants or tenure, ridiculed in journals which purport to be peer reviewed, and are often compared to holocaust deniers. But they ended this event up on their feet, cheering and unbowed, and ready to seek truth. They are determined to help end unnecessary climate-based fear being generated around the world. They want to put a stop to media manipulation of the world's populace, exemplified by an Australian TV program which encouraged children to figure out when their carbon footprint has been used up, and, therefore, they ought to die.

The conference program began with a rousing dinner address by the world's highest ranking political climate change skeptic, Czech Republic President Vaclav Klaus (currently also serving as President of the European Union). The "faculty" was comprised of Ph.D.s and area-specific experts from 14 nations. Lord Christopher Monckton, once the chief science advisor to Baroness Margaret Thatcher, and now Chief Policy Advisor for the UK Science and Public Policy Institute, brought the conference to end with a bravura speech.

One of the final panels included legendary "weatherman" John Coleman, whom many recall from the early days of ABC's "Good Morning America." It is no secret that Coleman -- who went on to become the founder of The Weather Channel -- is not a believer in the theory of man-made global warming. He regrets that The Weather Channel has succumbed to pressure to report climate falsehoods to the public. His presentation included the virtually unknown (might one say suppressed?) story of Al Gore's university professor whom Gore credits with triggering his interest in the planet. Dr. Roger Revelle came to recant the very research Gore (who received a C and a D in his only two college-level science courses) now uses as the basis for selling his carbon credit and cap and trade investment "opportunities." KUSI, the San Diego TV station on which Coleman appears these days, allowed him to report the full story. A video of the report was a part of his presentation. (watch the YouTube clip).

Also attending the Heartland event were two Irish film makers. During the previous week, Ann McElhinney and Phelim McAteer had the vast audience of approximately 8500 attendees at CPAC -- the Conservative Action Political Conference, in Washington D.C. -- standing and cheering. Their documentary, "Not Evil -- Just Wrong: The True Cost of Global Warming Hysteria," is brilliant. Among other things, it tells the story of why 40 million people, a large percentage of them African children, have died (some might even call it genocide) since the use of DDT was banned. The film details how the decision to ban DDT was based on the pseudo science -- offered up as fact -- in Rachel Carson's book, Silent Spring. Gore often cites Carson as his heroine. The film makes the obvious connections between them and the outcomes of their respective movements.

The problem is that "Not Evil- Just Wrong" is unlikely to air on any television network save Fox, although CSPAN would be smart to offer some air time. The plan is to go into shopping malls in an effort to reach the masses whose brains are being saturated with lies and misinformation designed to keep them frightened and malleable to politicians and self-interested elites. For more information, go to www.noteviljustwrong.com.

The good news is that the climate realists are gaining ground. 41% of respondents in a recent Gallop Poll said they thought global warming was "over hyped." 32,000 individuals, 10,000 of those with Ph.D.s in science, have now signed a new petition which calls into question tax payer funded mandated government policies -- and an array of guilt-based investment schemes -- which are based on flawed and distorted data being cited by global warming alarmists. This petition drive was led by Dr. Art Robinson of the Oregon Institute of Science and Medicine, who contributes to HUMAN EVENTS.

What is The Heartland Institute? For the past 25 years, Heartland has sought out free market solutions to challenges in all facets of our complex society. It gathers facts and data from the best sources available, functioning as a clearing house. It then provides detailed reports -- on a nonpartisan basis -- primarily to the 8,300 elected state and national officials in the U.S. Heartland claims that 8 out of every 10 elected officials now read Heartland's reports and use them when making policy decisions. This mandate has clearly never been more important. Talk about earth (and freedom and the future of world economics) being in the balance.

The entire Climate Change Conference -- every speaker, panel and power point presentation -- is now available online -- gratis -- at www.heartland.org.

March 25, 2009

G20 Road Show Comes to London

Any summit is practically over before it begins owing to the planning which goes into one, however brief. And this G20 meeting is beyond brief considering all the build up.

Here are some behind-the-scenes details.

Although it's known as the G20, British Prime Minister Gordon Brown has invited additional delegates from the Netherlands and Spain. A document purporting to be the guest host's official pecking order of nations was "leaked." Brazil, China, France, Germany, India, Italy, Japan, Saudi Arabia, South Africa, South Korea, and the United States make up the "A List." The "B" list nations are Canada, Australia, Russia, Argentina, Indonesia, Mexico and Turkey. The European Union, itself a member of the G20, suspiciously appears to be missing from the list.

Brown spent a part of Tuesday morning speaking about the ethics of globalization at Saint Paul's Cathedral, the iconic Wren edifice which survived the World War Two blitz. He reprised the Martin Luther King line about "the fierce urgency of now," quoted often during the Obama Presidential campaign. With all Brown has riding on this summit, he most certainly fervently prayed as well.

The Queen and Prince Philip will host a reception on Wednesday evening. Every country attending the G20 was allowed to bring five people. Later, at the Prime Minster's residence, Number 10 Downing Street, celebrity chef, Jaime Oliver will oversee the serving of his dinner menu to the inner circle of leaders. He might have an extra helping left over if President Sarkozy of France makes good on his threat to walk out of the summit. Sarko has his own agenda -- creation of a new global financial czar. He was recently heard to sniff that he should get his way because this financial mess was all the fault of "les Anglo-Saxons."

Meanwhile, the police and diverse groups of protestors were having their own run-up to the big day. A few days ago, five people were arrested on suspicion of planning to disrupt the summit. A flurry of police raids disgorged explosives made of fireworks and an array of weapons from handguns to hunting rifles to a Kalashnikov-style assault rifle.

A group calling itself "The G20 Meltdown" took charge of co-coordinating four different marches that are supposed to converge on the Bank of England. To keep things coordinated, the organizers have set up a Twitter account. Several groups who call themselves anarchists have announced they will join one or more of the scheduled marches, but will break away once in the City of London (aka The Square Miles aka The Financial District). A map labeled "Squaring up to the Square Mile" has been circulated among protesters, but someone has observed that the location it gives for London Stock Exchange is incorrect. The LSE relocated in 2004 and is now across the street from Saint Paul's Cathedral.

The protestors have also previewed their official souvenir for the day. It is a fake British Bank Note with a nasty depiction of the Scottish economist and moral philosopher, Adam Smith, on one side and a faceless jester in place of the Queen on the other. The idea is to litter the City with the gag currency, which one presumes is to show their concern for the environment, if not the trees.

More than 3,000 police officers will be on duty during the summit period, with up to 10,000 protesters expected to stage rallies and marches. A new reinforced ring of steel has been constructed around the U.S. embassy in central London. The Foreign Office has said that the summit is likely to cost the British government around £20 million. £8 million of that amount will be for security.

Now as for President Obama's participation in the summit, the White House has not released an estimated cost to the U.S. taxpayer, but it must enough to bail out another bank or two. The

President landed at Stansted Airport on Tuesday evening aboard Air Force One, along with the First Lady, 200 members of the American secret service and another 300 staffers -- the Portable White House if you will. It is the largest travelling retinue in U.S. presidential history. The President's limo, nicknamed "The Beast" for its extremely elaborate security add-ons, was flown over. A couple of helicopters were necessary too, and so was the ubiquitous press corps. The UK Telegraph's U.S. Editor, Toby Harnden, was among the media band on Air Force One. He received a copy of what he described as a sort of "Britain for Dummies Guide" with the Presidential seal on it. Did you know that Britain is slightly smaller than Oregon?

Upon his arrival, the President was met by Chancellor (Treasury Secretary Equivalent), Alistair Darling and his wife Margaret. No bands. The British public were informed that, being aware of the current economic realities, Mr. Darling travelled to the airport on the Stansted Express Train from London's Liverpool Street Station, accompanied by a few police officers and security staff. It has also been revealed that the gift bags assembled for the G20 have been downsized, with a classic British Tea Towel as the signature gift item.

Ironically, the Obamas will be staying at the official residence of the U.S. ambassador. Winfield House was built in the 1930s (during the last Great Depression) with money inherited from retailer Franklin Winfield Woolworth. Woolworth's (UK) went belly-up last year, after a century of being Britain's most beloved five and ten store.

On Thursday morning, the world leaders finally get down to work at the Excel centre in London's docklands. Here is the schedule:

Leaders' breakfast: 8:30 a.m.-9:45 a.m.
Morning session including finance ministers and central bankers: 9:50 a.m.-1:25pm
Lunch: 1:25 p.m. - 2:30 p.m.
Afternoon session including finance ministers and central bankers: 2:30 p.m.-3:30 p.m.
Closing press conferences: 3:30 onwards

That's it!

All that time and trouble and money for this select group of people to get together in London to solve the world's financial crisis, and the taxpayers of the world won't even get eight hours of labor out of them. If fixing the ailing global economy was only going to take four hours and 35 minutes of work, punctuated with lavish meals, couldn't they have done it more easily, sooner, and more economically? Whatever happened to energy efficiency and global warming concerns? What's wrong with eco-friendly video teleconferencing?

Pass me a tea towel. I need to have a good cry.

April 1, 2009

Tales from Obama's Grand Tour -- Did You Miss These Stories?

For two centuries, the upper classes of Europe -- and eventually wealthy Americans -- engaged in a requisite journey to the great capitals of the continent. This was known as "The Grand Tour." The goal was to imbue the traveler with a respect for history and the cultural achievements of previous civilizations. It was a test of one's social graces.

How did President Obama do on his Grand Tour? Here are some media markers.

A reporter in the Netherlands likened the reception Obama received to the way Gorbachev was initially -- enthusiastically -- welcomed by the Warsaw Pact countries in the late 80's. The BBC surprisingly probed "Beyond the Obama Magic." The German publication, der Spiegel, observed that the visit did not portend a new world order. A French pundit, referred to Obama's desire to end nuclear proliferation as naïve "theology." And Turkish TV News anchor Gokhan Taskin -- known as "the Glenn Beck of Turkey" -- created quite an uproar when he delivered a message to Obama in black-face make-up. Translated from Turkish, what Taskin said was: "Welcome Mr. Obama. You took our hearts with your hospitality. We appreciate your kindness. We will do whatever America asks of us, as friends. Now we ask the same of you." Not exactly incendiary satire.

Here is some other news you might have missed.

Mr. Obama's surprise visit to Baghdad was the equivalent of dropping by for a quick cup of tea and a photo op. He underscored his desire to have US troops leave as soon as possible so the US could turn things over the Iraqis. What didn't get much attention from the US media was a plea from the Archbishop of Kirkuk, Louis Sako. He wants the troops to stay because their departure puts Iraqi Christians at increased risk. Five have been murdered in the last month alone. Sako believes that once the US withdraws, Iraq will disintegrate into violence and possible civil war because "ethnic and religious groups have not become truly reconciled and the security situation remains fragile."

A Chaldean Catholic Bishop in Mosul explained that members of the Christian community are being targeted by organized crime groups because of the wealth they have created -- "built up in a lifetime of toil and sweat" -- through their commercial enterprises. Sounds vaguely familiar.

In the past, he explained, "these thugs were covered and protected by al-Qaeda, but now that the ideological and confessional element is disappearing, ordinary criminals and organized crime [groups] are rearing their head, drawn by money, ready to kill in cold blood." Sounds sort of like Somali pirates.

One presumes that the Archbishop did not hear President Obama tell an audience in Turkey that America is no longer just a Christian nation, a comment Obama first tested out on the campaign trail to mixed reviews. To deliver that statement in a Muslim country during Holy Week struck some Christians as insensitive at best. Domestic news stories about the Obamas' scramble to find a church to attend on Easter Sunday, and the unprecedented hosting of a Passover Seder at The White House, helped reinforce the idea that the President is "interfaith," and therefore perhaps not inclined to worry unduly about the death toll of his policies on Iraqi Christians.

The US media also fast forwarded through footage of the anti-American demonstrations mounted in Turkey. They did not coincide with the idea that once George Bush was gone, all anti-American sentiments would vanish. Not so. There were huge protests against his visit in many Turkish cities. And leave it to Al Jazeera to remind us that Bill Clinton was the first US President to address the Turkish Parliament, in 1996. No precedent breaker there for Obama.

Meanwhile, back in the USA, an Armenian-American group which had helped elect Obama was upset with him for not taking a more forceful position on the Armenian genocide, committed by the Turks during World War I. Even National Public Radio host, Scott Simon, opined that it was insufficient to label the deaths of 1.5 million people as just "killings." Apparently Obama enlisted the assistance of Swiss negotiators to help resolve this thorny issue. Having the parties come to terms with this tragic history is a hurdle which must be cleared before Turkey can be accepted into the European Union.

Here the President of France makes one of his many appearances in the historical record of Obama's Grand Tour. Nicholas Sarkozy does not want the EU to embrace Turkey. Period. Although Sarko threatened (but did not) boycott the G-20 meeting, he is not kidding about blocking Turkey's entrance into the EU. He as much as told Obama to "fergettaboutit." For a start, Sarkozy can do the math. Since Turkey is a Muslim nation -- albeit allegedly "secular" -- the fact is that once Turkish residents are added into the EU, the European Union will become 10% Muslim. It would give meaning to the old adage about why one should not allow the camel to get his nose under your tent flap. The rest of the camel will soon follow.

Sarkozy was also none too pleased that the exquisite town of Strasbourg was hit by anti-NATO protests while -- just across the bridge on the German side of the border -- things remained calm. Perhaps this explains why he chose to send in special operations troops and risk a rescue of French tourists when they were held hostage by Somali pirates. One hostage was killed, as were all but one of the pirates, and you can bet his trial will become a major media event in France. The object was that Sarko took action while Obama and Hillary Clinton were pictured meeting at the picnic table next to the new swing set in the White House grounds. Point -- Counterpoint.

Winding back to the beginning, there has been much made of the IPod which the President gave the Queen. What does it say about a man who calls his country "arrogant," after he has just given the Queen of England audio copies of his best and most memorable speeches? She has seen eleven US Presidents come and go and none did anything quite so tacky. Even worse -- Obama returned a special gift -- loaned by the British Empire to The White House after 9-11. It was a bronze bust of Winston Churchill worth hundreds of thousands of British pounds. Although he was told the White House was welcome to hold on to it, Obama flew Winston back to England. Here's the beef. When Churchill was in power, Britain suppressed the Mau Mau Rebellion in Kenya, birthplace of Mr. Obama's father. The President's grandfather, Hussein Onyango Obama, is thought to have been among those tortured by British colonial forces.

The problem is protocol. When Michelle Obama spontaneously gave the Queen a wee backrub during the G-20 reception at Buckingham Palace, the joke was that "even Prince Philip doesn't get to do that." Returning the prized bust, even if it was to settle an old family score, was done in such a way that the press had a heads-up. But why?

Discretion is often the better part of diplomacy, which one hopes is what Mr. Obama has now learned after his "Grand Tour." It's a dubious hope.

April 14, 2009

UK Government Official Caught in Internet Plot to Smear Opposing Party

There are NO, repeat NO domestic problems in England. It is still the fabled fair green isle it ever was. The people live like kings and queens -- with no small number of well fed peasants -- all cohabiting in a perfect society: harmonious, healthy, with all future prospects rosy and abundant.

That's why Prime Minster Gordon Brown's staff at Number Ten Downing Street have nothing to do. Well, they might have been able to watch the DVDs which Obama gave Brown as gifts, but they are incompatible with UK electronic standards. What's that about arrogance? But I digress.

During the first week in April -- when the G-20 was meeting in London -- the British media got wind of a wicked story. The leaking of this story is now itself the focus of controversial crossfire between reporters from the UK Telegraph and a conservative political blog, www.order-order.com, a website honoring Guy Fawkes. Fawkes was the leader of a plot to blow up Parliament in the late 16th century and is remembered every November 5 -- with firework displays -- for his efforts. Order-Order calls him the last man to enter Parliament with honest intentions.

This 21st century plot involved the creation of an explosive political blog. The man behind it was identified as Derek Draper, a political hack with an odd resume. The project was being shepherded along by Prime Minister Gordon Brown's Head of Strategy and Planning, Damian McBride. The anonymous -- seemingly independent -- blog was to be named Red Rag. Its sole function was to post vile rumors about the sex lives of conservative politicians, including the leader of the Tory Party, David Cameron. This slimy jaw-dropping plan was exposed just a few weeks after Gordon

Brown delivered a moving eulogy -- in Parliament -- to mark the passing of Cameron's young son. Ivan, age 6, had just died from complications related to birth defects.

In retrospect, this scene now seems chilling because Red Rag's initial edition planned to falsely report that the grieving David Cameron had once gone to a private doctor who secretly treated sexual diseases for socially prominent people.

When Red Rag's existence and purpose came to light, the public was truly revolted. The obvious question was the extent of Brown's prior knowledge and approval of the blog. The fallout has become known as "Smeargate." Damian McBride resigned the day the story went public. He had no choice. E-mails between McBride and Draper about Red Rag were sent and received from a computer located in the Press Office of Number Ten Downing Street. Closing the barn door after the horse had escaped, Brown made a Cabinet Secretary write up a statement on how policy advisors ought to behave just after McBride was ejected from the inner circle. Conservative MP Nadine Dorries, who learned she was to be smeared on Red Rag, has since a filed a lawsuit against McBride.

Yet despite Brown's repeated denials that he knew anything about the sordid plan, let alone felt he needed to apologize to anyone, Smeargate would not go away so easily, primarily because this was not the first "Gate" in which Red Rag's creator had been a player.

In the early days of the Labour Government, as led by Tony Blair, Derek Draper (then a young political neophyte with delusions of grandeur) boasted to an undercover reporter from the Observer newspaper that he was "intimate" with at least 17 influential people in the Labour Party and could make things happen -- like selling access to certain ministers.

When this interview transcript was made public, Draper's boasts were all denied by Labour Party members and the braggart left London. He landed in Berkeley, Calif., where he later claimed to have earned a Master's Degree in Clinical Psychology. Back in London after three years in the once Golden State, Draper set up shop as a private therapist and wrote articles on psychology for the newspapers. He also married a comely hostess of the UK equivalent (GMTV) of Good Morning America and began reinserting himself into Labour's power circles. But his track record made a blogger from the left leaning Guardian (the Observer's sister publication) suspicious. It was discovered that Draper had lied about attending the University of California, Berkeley. He was forced to amend his story and said he had actually attended The Wright Institute in Berkeley. This was not a lie, but Wright said Draper was asked to leave the campus three years into its five year graduate program. The reason for the Institute's action has not been revealed.

Undaunted by the disclosure of his deceit, Draper kept looking for ways to insinuate himself back into the Labour Party. He soon decided that the Internet could be his ticket to being perceived as an influential player. He created www.LabourList.org, reinventing himself as an electronic tabloid political guru. Despite McBride's full and complete knowledge of Draper's past (his story is detailed in a Wikipedia entry as well as in newspaper archives), Brown's strategy man, McBride, encouraged the launch of the Red Rag blog.

Echoes of the original "Gate" scandal swirled around Brown as they had around Nixon. If Brown did know, he was guilty. If he didn't, he was incompetent. There has since been a call for inquiries into how people like Derek Draper and Damian McBride are allowed to operate as outside consultants within Number Ten Downing Street, and how anyone is to believe they could do anything which is not at their master's bidding and with his blessing. Hard to imagine what conclusions will be reached, eh?

Worried about becoming tarnished by association, former Labour government ministers began telling the press that Brown was clearly to blame for this fiasco. They put it down to his leadership style -- one in which this kind of "freelancing" flourished. When David Cameron asserted this incident indicated an urgent shake-up of the Downing Street machine was necessary, many members of the Labour Party became his hallelujah chorus. Draper has now been banned from all Labour Party events, but unbelievably he is out and about promoting his new book, Life Support, with his very pregnant talking head wife by his side. He has his own blog which invites folks to listen to his media interviews and view all of his "red carpet appearances." He is the one trying to look like a Bono clone.

Gordon Brown eventually mumbled a sort of apology for Red Rag, adding that he was "horrified" and "very angry" about the whole affair. But if you assume the Prime Minister was put in his place by this current public humiliation, think again. In the past week, the new Labour government budget has just been unveiled. The top income tax rate has been raised to the 50 percent level. And to address the revelation that many MPs were renting out the homes they got rent free for their government service, Brown proposed that elected officials should, instead, now each receive a daily payment of £150 for showing up to work in London, on top of their salaries and other perks.

By the week's end, rumors that a rift existed between Brown and his Exchequer (Treasury Secretary) Alistair Darling were essentially confirmed by Darling himself. Darling says he knew the budget figures he presented to Parliament "didn't add up" and argued with Brown in favor of making far deeper, deficit reducing, cuts in government spending. Brown overruled Darling, fearing that further cutbacks would cause Labour to lose the next national election. He may have a point. England is definitely a welfare state.

A Times of London story just reported that: "nearly eight million people of working age in Britain have been "economically inactive" for the past few years. More than 2.5 million of them are on incapacity benefit - of these 2,130 people are too "fat" to work; 1,100 can't work because they have trouble getting to sleep; 4,000 get headaches; 380 are confined to the sofa by hemorrhoids; 3,000 are kept at home by gout; and half a million are too depressed to get a job. According to Dame Carol Black, the National Director of

Health and Work, one child in five now comes from a family where neither parent works, yet at the end of last year there were half a million job vacancies."

A general election must be called by next spring. Bookmakers are now giving the Conservatives a numerical triple leap in the winning odds. Will voters choose to try to save the Empire or let it continue to crumble?

April 30, 2009

Europeans Rate Obama

There are those who think it does not matter what Europeans think of America, but Barack Obama made wooing Europeans a cornerstone of his campaign for the presidency. Thus it seems fair game to ask -- how did the European press rate his first 100 days in office?

The Daily Mail Online had the most provocative headline: "Obamamania or Overkill?" It attached many of the exclusive photos which Obama had taken to commemorate this benchmark in his Presidency. The first showed the President in the private White House movie theater watching the Super Bowl with friends. Seeing the leader of the free world (an arguably applicable title these days) in 3-D glasses made for an odd image. Then there were photos of Obama walking the family's new dog, Obama rearranging furniture, Obama tossing a football in the Oval Office, Obama putting on the White House green, Obama shooting hoops in the equivalent of his driveway, and lots of endearing Obama family snaps.

Britain not having the best reputation for its cuisine, the Mail's article made much ado about how butterfly-shaped Pepperidge Farm crackers are favored by the President for his snacks. Those who wished to emulate this nibbling option were informed that Pepperidge Farm had "not yet dented the UK markets." Really? Whatever happened to globalization?

Charles Hawley, writing for the more taciturn der Spiegel, said that Obama had already discredited himself -- and his country -- by not being able to deal with various issues related to the prisoners held in Guantanamo, adding that "German commentators are disappointed." To illustrate his point, Hawley cited articles from several papers across the political spectrum. The bottom line is that the Germans think Obama's inability to devolve Gitmo breaks some sort faith they had in his ability to change things.

Another der Spiegel article, "The Instant American Revolution," began by informing readers that it was Franklin Roosevelt who instituted the arbitrary 100-day mark, calling it an "artificial anniversary" akin to the Korean tradition of celebrating a baby's birth after 100 days. But despite referring to the "know it alls on the right" who diss Obama at every turn, this article goes on to warn Obama not to coast on the polls which show he is turning the mood of the nation around (although another Daily Mail article asserts Obama poll numbers have actually fallen below those of Clinton's early days).

Despite his personal popularity, the new President is reminded here that he is being watched for his actual policy decisions. It is also clear that Europeans are aware of Obama's cabinet and staffing problems (and this was before the infamous New York City flyover). The "Worms in the Apple" list is topped by Timothy Geithner, while Larry Summers is identified as "the personification of pessimism."

Valentina Pop, writing for The EUobserver, suggests that President Obama has failed to fill in the blanks in his policies toward Eastern Europe and Russia. Despite his meetings with the leaders in this bloc, and his obvious difference in style from George Bush, insiders report his actual positions on a variety of issues are "vague." She quotes Michael Emerson from the Centre for European Policy Studies (identified as a centre-right think tank) who suggests Obama needs more time to get his administration in order.

The Italian Prime Minster, billionaire Silvio Berlusconi -- embroiled in a nasty divorce -- was too busy to contribute to the 100-day commentaries. It is, however, somewhat telling that since meeting Obama at the G-20 Summit, Mr. Berlusconi announced to the world's press that he (not Obama) was indisputably the Jesus Christ of Italian (if not world) politics. "I'm a patient victim. I put up with everything. I sacrifice myself for everyone," he said. One can see how the painting of Obama as a Christ figure -- unveiled to coincide with the 100-day mark -- might have bruised Berlusconi tender ego.

This caused the usually mild-mannered Pope Benedict to tell the Prime Minister to pipe down.

The British Broadcasting Company (BBC) asked three (cleverly selected) international political cartoonists to characterize Obama's first 100 days.

Hozhaber Shinwary of Afghanistan said his focus was on the change of having US foreign policy run by the State Department, and no longer by the US military. His image of Obama had the president walking on a very fine rope between the White House and the rest of the world. His message for Obama, said Shinwary, was that he could easily slip into a dangerous world below him.

Nikahang Kowsar of Iran chose to portray Mr. Obama as the Greek mythological character, Sisyphus, trying -- unsuccessfully -- to roll the globe up a hill and prevent it from rolling down, only to be impaled on a financial graph with all indicators spiking down. Ouch. Noting that Bush was at least funny, Kowsar said "a cartoonist usually has an opinion and, personally, I'm not sure he (Obama) can deliver. How this squares with Obama's idea that he can make a diplomatic breakthrough with Iran is open to debate.

Finally, Rayma Suprani from Venezuela chose to illustrate Obama's first 100 days with a cartoon strip showing our President's recent meeting with Venezuelan President (for life?) Hugo Chavez. He portrays Mr. Obama as asking someone "Do you want to be my friend?" The next cartoon frame shows that Obama is actually addressing Bo, the family's new pet dog and in the last frame, the dog accepts the offer. "You can interpret that however you like," Kowsar concluded.

This is not to say that Obama does not maintain his "magic" among certain Europeans -- the regular folks. For example, Prince Charles is organizing a fresh and new campaign to save the rainforests so he just hired the Internet consultancy firm which created the website for Obama's Presidential campaign. It has been noted that Charles does not email, or use a Blackberry. Nor does he have an iPhone; - although his Mom could surely share the iPod Obama gave her recently just to help her eldest son get more tech friendly. It is not as if iPhones endanger rainforests. But what this whole deal indicates is that it is business as usual. The elites continue to faithfully hire one another so at least one employment sector is safe from the recession.

With his own poll ratings rolling downhill, French President Nicholas Sarkozy has announced a major photo op for himself and Obama. This will take place on June 6th, on the Normandy beaches, at the 65th anniversary of the D-Day landings which led to the liberation of Nazi-occupied France.

One wonders if -- on that occasion -- some French political cartoonist will portray Sarkozy as an American poodle (an image frequently used to illustrate Tony Blair's relationship to George Bush). Or will there be a sketch showing Obama asking a canine caricature of Sarkozy if he wants to be his friend?

May 12, 2009

A Tale of Two Speakers

What the Dickens is happening? It must be open season on House Speakers.

On May 19, for the first time in three centuries, the speaker of the House of Commons (of the Parliament of the United Kingdom of Great Britain and Northern Ireland), resigned his post. Michael Martin was told to fall on his sword by British Prime Minister Gordon Brown a few weeks after records of scandalous expense claims -- made by of Members of Parliament from all parties -- were leaked to The Daily Telegraph. Incontrovertible proof in hand, the Telegraph printed the sordid details.

Outrage ensued. The Queen scolded Brown during their weekly meeting. David Cameron, leader of the Conservatives, went so far as to insist that any Tory who did not repay falsified expenses drawn on the public purse would be kicked out of the Party. The clamor reached a fever pitch when -- on Monday's live TV coverage of the Parliament session -- Martin found himself facing down an angry sea of MPs. It made for compelling, albeit uncomfortable, viewing.

While Martin has been under fire, controversy has simultaneously been swirling around U.S. Speaker of the House, Nancy Pelosi. This strange bit of political parallelism is the stuff of novels. It is a tale about commoners and kings (or in this case a queen).

Here are the two plots.

Two Different Backgrounds:

Michael Martin was born in Scotland in 1945, the son of an alcoholic merchant seaman and a school cleaner. He grew up in a Glasgow tenement with four brothers and sisters. The toilet was outside. He left school at 15 to apprentice as a sheet metal worker and joined the Labour Party at age 21. After proving himself as a trade union organizer, Martin was elected to represent a Glasgow constituency in 1979.

Nancy D'Alesandro was born, in 1940, into a prominent family which -- for many years -- ran the Democrat political machine in Maryland. Her father, Tommy D'Alesandro, Jr., was a U.S. Congressman. He and Nancy's brother each served terms as Mayor of Baltimore. She attended a Catholic girl's school and entered Trinity College, where she met her husband, Paul Pelosi. The newly weds moved to the San Francisco Bay area.

The Pelosi family currently has a net worth of nearly $19 million, earned through real estate, including a winery, stocks and other investments. Nancy Pelosi is the ninth wealthiest member of the House. She holds the record for the most financial contributions to the campaigns of other Democrats because her own seat has been so secure.

Two Different Paths to Power

Not having his skids greased by being from the upper class, Michael Martin MP climbed up the ranks of the Labour Party by chairing a host of committees for little glory. U.K. tradition calls for the Speakership to alternate from one party to the other whenever the post is open. Martin maneuvered himself into the opening despite his predecessor being a Labourite. He became Speaker of the House of Commons in October 2000.

Pelosi became involved in San Francisco politics as a high society lady, working her way up to become California State Party Chairwoman by 1977. A decade later, when the last of her five children was a high school senior, she decided to run for office.

After her election to the House in 1987, Pelosi also did her fair share of committee work, but these were not without glory. She served on both the Appropriations and -- more importantly -- the House Intelligence Committee, eventually become the ranking Democrat. She remained on that Committee until becoming the Minority Leader of the House. She was elected Speaker by the House Democrat majority in January 2007.

Two Different Sets of Responsibilities

The Speaker of the U.S. House of Representatives serves as the presiding officer of that body. The Commons Speakers is also supposed to keep the house in order.

Pelosi is second in the line of Presidential succession after the vice president. No such opportunity for advancement exists in the House of Commons, although Martin regularly interacted with the Queen on pertinent matters.

Congresswoman Pelosi is allowed to be a partisan advocate for the Democrat Party while being House Speaker. The British Speaker is supposed to be impartial and independent of government, but Martin also retained his seat as a Labour MP.

The Speaker of the Commons is referred to as First Commoner of the Land. Try calling Nancy Pelosi "common."

Two Different Reputations

Michael Martin has a reputation for having a chip on his shoulder. He is said to have charged the taxpayers for postage when he mailed his dirty underwear home -- to Scotland -- for his wife to launder.

A senior Democrat once described Pelosi as "our Maggie Thatcher," which must have made her cringe. Others call her a "diva." Her staff got bad press for treating the Air Force as Pelosi's personal airline service, berating military officials in several emails. This prompted Judicial Watch President Tom Fitton to remark, "Her office seems unconcerned about wasting taxpayer money with last minute travel cancellations and other demands."

Two Different Controversies

Michael Martin actively attempted to block Freedom of Information requests which would have exposed the horrific billings, charged to the public coffers, by members of Parliament and of the government.

Nancy Pelosi has issued five different sets of explanations about what she knew or didn't know about water boarding and other interrogation techniques. She has since accused the CIA of lying to her.

Two Different Outcomes?

Michael Martin will step down on June 21. He is due a pension of £1.4million and is supposed to receive a peerage. He'll get the pension, but the title issue is being hotly debated. He did not want to go, especially in disgrace. He still denies any direct ethical responsibility for the culture of corruption he presided over.

In an unprecedented action, Former House Speaker, Newt Gingrich, has called for Speaker Pelosi to resign. So far, she has avoided being pilloried by an angry House on C-SPAN, but the current CIA chief, long-time Democrat partisan Leon Panetta, has all but called her a liar. Insiders say he never would have done that without first running it up Rahm Emanuel's flagpole. There are rumblings that the long knives in the White House and on Capitol Hill are out for her.

The question is: Will Nancy Pelosi be forced to step down from her position? (Let's not even try to calculate her pension). In addition to those testy intelligence briefings, as a part of the Obama administration, Pelosi is also open to scrutiny as regards the out of control federal budget. The voters of California just sent a big warning shot across the bow over government extravagance and waste. Will Americans rise up in righteous indignation the way the British have over the Expenses Scandal in Parliament -- threatening to vote out everyone on the guilty list? Can Nancy Pelosi still find her moral voice or will she be disgraced? Is her season over? Therein hangs the tale.

May 26, 2009

EU Parliamentary Elections Send Mixed Signals. Moving Right or Acting Out?

If one looks only at the end result, the headlines are generally correct. Last weekend's elections for seats in the EU Parliament indicate power in that body is now concentrated to the right of center. But things are never that simple when 27 countries are involved in creating a super-state entity while – simultaneously – being embroiled in their own national political dramas.

For a start, who exactly is moving anything in any direction when only 43.09 percent of all eligible voters go to the polls? 10 out of the 27 EU nations recorded higher turnouts, with Belgium and Luxembourg on the high end at 91 percent. Three former Soviet satellites (the Czech Republic, Lithuania and Slovakia) came in on the low end at 25 percent or under. It would seem that the €18 million ($25 mil) the EU Parliament spent on an "election awareness campaign" was not a good civic investment. Of course, bureaucracies are famous for squandering the people's money.

To the uninitiated, European Party politics can be confusing. Here is a brief introduction. The EU Parliament now comprises 736 seats. These seats are currently held among seven parties and a miscellaneous segment known as "Others." To be listed on an EU Parliamentary ballot and submit candidates for election, a party must meet basic EU requirements by holding a certain percentage of seats within its own national government. All 27 EU countries vote on candidates from within their own nations by party affiliation. The final configuration of the EU Parliament is, therefore, a reflection of the distribution of elected party members when the ballots from each nation are tallied and added together.

The number of party members elected by each country can also create a power base. Germany will be sending 99 deputies to

Belgium, the largest national contingent, since Chancellor Angela Merkel's Christian Democrat Party crushed its competition, the Social Democrats, by a margin of 48 to 20.8 percent. In France, President Sarkozy's Union for a Popular Movement received 28 percent of the vote as compared to 16.8 percent for the Socialists, but France's voter turnout was below the overall average of 43 percent. What these figures suggest is that rather than turning to the right, Europeans turned away from voting at all and clearly the Socialists were more likely to sit this one out.

So is Europe really moving right? You decide. Whereas the US has two major parties who essentially divvy up the power, the EU Parliament is diversity defined. For the purposes of EU elections, coalitions of like minded parties come together under umbrella names and identities, coagulating around core issues and shared policies. Here are the Parties, their relative positions on the political spectrum, and the number of seats they now hold.

* The EPP-ED (Group of European People's Party) is a centre-right umbrella coalition which won a total of 265 seats. EPP-affiliated parties govern France, Germany, Italy and Poland.

* The PES, or Socialist Group, came in second place with 184 seats.

* UEN (Union for Europe of the Nations) Supports the EU Constitution, but can be conservative on the national level.

* ALDE (Alliance of Liberals and Democrats for Europe) won 83 seats. These are centrists who hold the key to the left/right balance of power.

* Greens/EFA (Group of the Greens European Free Alliance) won 50 seats. This group consists of ecologically minded representatives from stateless nations or "regionalists." They lobby for sustainable development, fundamental human rights, and environmental justice.

* GUE/NGL (Confederated Group of the European United Left and Nordic Green Left) won 36 seats. Consists of members from 17 parties in 13 European countries, all firmly committed to European integration, but not along the lines of the current EU model. They are "anti neo monetarists" who favor conferences between national parliaments in addition to maintaining an EU Parliament separately.

* IND/DEM (Independence Democracy Group) won 21 seats. This coalition consists of EU-critics, eurosceptics and eurorealists who reject establishing a constitution for Europe and oppose all forms of centralization. The UK Independence Party (very anti-EU) falls into this group.

Then there are the "OTHERS" who won 72 seats. Who might they be? Here are three notable examples.

Suggesting an anti-Muslim backlash is on the upswing in the Netherlands, winning 17 percent of the Dutch vote, the Party for Freedom secured four seats. This is the party of the anti-Islamic activist lawmaker Geert Wilders.

This result was echoed in Austria where the rightist Freedom Party - which also campaigned on an anti- Islam platform, more than doubled its strength from the 2004 elections receiving 13.1 percent of the vote.

In the United Kingdom, the British National Party won its first two EU seats. The BNP is considered so "ultra right" that Conservative Party leader, David Cameron, describes them as "beyond the pale."

Garnering 7 percent of their nation's vote, Sweden's Pirate Party won a seat. This group campaigned for the legalization of Internet file sharing, the reformation of other copyright and patent laws, and an end to government authorized monitoring of emails.

The bottom line is – despite these breakout party results - mainstream center-left parties still hold between 155 to 165 seats in the EU Parliament and the right in Europe is still primarily just right of center, not off the revolutionary charts.

It remains to be seen how all these disparate groups will ever be able to legislate, not altogether a bad thing if one subscribes to the idea that people are safer when elected bodies are not in session. It might be better (and far more cost effective) if the Parliament was more like the US Senate, with two persons chosen to represent each nation, but it is not the Republic of Europe, it is the European Union, and primarily a democratic union at that,

Something must be said about the actual EU voting process. It was held over four days, with the British and Dutch going first on Thursday June 4th and voters from 19 out of the 27 EU nations -- including France, Germany, Italy and Spain – casting their ballots on June 7th. It seems no coincidence that the anniversary of "The Longest Day" took place over what seemed to be the longest balloting weekend ever. There were no hanging chads, nor complaints about precinct hi-jinks – but - there was a tacit agreement that the nations which voted first would keep their results under wraps so as not to suggest any trends. No such luck.

The turmoil facing the governing Labour Party government in the UK spilled into EU balloting, further eroding the nearly non existent authority of Prime Minister Gordon Brown. The Dutch results were reported on-the-spot as proof of that nation's current polarized and tense state of political affairs.

Still – kudos to the fact that 27 distinct countries could hold elections to a common governing body and have the final results tallied with such breath taking speed. Color graphics of the results were available on the EU Parliament's own website not two hours after the last of the polls closed. The EU Parliament has also copied C-SPAN and will soon have its own TV channel as a part of the movement toward greater transparency.

Let's hope it's like watching a docudrama, not a sitcom.

June 9, 2009